Chosen
With
Purpose

A Story of Adoption & Identity

MARK MOLZEN

ISBN: 1480151297
ISBN-13: 9781480151291
Library Of Congress Control Number: 2013912739

CreateSpace Independent Publishing Platform,
North Charleston, South Carolina

DEDICATION

For my father, mother, three sisters, and two brothers
— the "United Nations" of adoption

and

To every adopted child — both young and old —
who struggles with his or her identity, worth, and purpose

CONTENTS

ACKNOWLEDGMENTS

~ To God, who made me who I am and allowed me to be adopted —
twice ~

~ To my mother, who always told me I could write, and
to my father, who gave me the discipline to make it happen ~

~ To my wife, who is my best friend, and the mother of our three
amazing boys ~

SPECIAL THANKS TO

Colin and Cindy Molzen
David Schumaker
Dawn Ehresman
Eric Falkner
James C. Wangerin
Mike and Julie Gowans
Milt Ferrantelli
Odell Riley
Olivia Wolf
Troy Fullwood

INTRODUCTION

The subject of adoption conjures up many images — some positive and some negative. With approximately five million adoptees in America today, adoption has become mainstream. However, there remains a certain stigma both within the adoption community and outside of it. My question is, why?

The family I grew up in was not a typical family, in size or makeup. There were six of us kids in all. Someone once told us we represented all the colors of the rainbow — our own rainbow coalition of sorts. My parents had two biological and four adopted children, but in our family, that meant my parents had six kids *of their own*.

Within our family we came pretty close to representing all the major continents. I have brothers and sisters who are European American, Native American, Asian American, and African American. We also made a run at covering the Gospels; we have a Matthew, Mark, and Luke in our family. I believe that at one time we started calling our cat John, but it didn't take. Regarding adoption, in our family we were all-in.

As I think about how adoption is viewed today, I often shake my head. Adoption is joked about and even used as a punch line when someone does something strange or out of the ordinary ("Oh, they must be adopted."). I believe we need a fundamental change in how people think about adoption, in how adults who have been adopted feel about themselves, and in how we explain to children what being adopted means. Although I am not a doctor or a counselor, I feel I have a unique perspective on adoption. After all, I've been adopted twice.

So how is adoption defined today? The *Merriam-Webster Online Dictionary* defines adoption as

> **to take by choice** into a relationship; *especially*: to take voluntarily (a child of other parents) as one's own child…to accept formally…**to choose**[1]

At Dictionary.com you will find the following definitions:

From the *World English Dictionary* (Collins)

> 1. *law* to bring (a person) into a specific relationship, esp to take (another's child) as one's own child 2. **to choose** and follow (a plan, technique, etc.) 3. to take over (an idea, etc.) as if it were one's own 4. to take on; assume: *to adopt a title* 5. **to accept** (a report, etc.) [C16: from Latin *adoptāre* to choose for oneself, from *optāre* **to choose**][2]

From the *Illustrated Bible Dictionary* (Easton):

---

[1] *Merriam-Webster Online Dictionary*, s.v. "adopt," http://www.merriam-webster.com/dictionary/adopt (emphasis in bold added).
[2] *World English Dictionary* (Collins), 10th ed., s.v. "adopt," http://dictionary.reference.com/browse/adopt?s=t.

Adoption: the giving to any one the name and place and privileges of a son who is not a son by birth.

Natural. Thus Pharaoh's daughter adopted Moses (Exodus 2:10), and Mordecai Esther (Esther 2:7).

National. God adopted Israel (Exodus 4:22; Deuteronomy 7:6; Hosea 11:1; Romans 9:4).

Spiritual. An act of God's grace by which he brings men into the number of his redeemed family, and makes them partakers of all the blessings he has provided for them. Adoption represents the new relations into which the believer is introduced by justification, and the privileges connected therewith, viz., an interest in God's peculiar love (John 17:23; Romans 5:5-8), a spiritual nature (2 Peter 1:4; John 1:13), the possession of a spirit becoming children of God (1 Peter 1:14; 2 John 4; Romans 8:15-21; Galatians 5:1; Hebrews 2:15), present protection, consolation, supplies (Luke 12:27-32; John 14:18; 1 Corinthians 3:21-23; 2 co [sic] 1:4), fatherly chastisements (Hebrews 12:5-11), and a future glorious inheritance (Romans 8:17 Romans 8:23; James 2:5; Philippians 3:21).[3]

Those of us who are adopted, who have adopted children, or who are considering adoption know that *adoption* means so much more than any dictionary entry could cover. At its core, adoption involves a plan, a choice, and acceptance. The reality is that we've all been adopted spiritually in Christ, according to God's plan for salvation, and we all have to accept that it was God's plan that we be adopted into His family and not our own.

---

[3] *Illustrated Bible Dictionary* (Easton), 3rd ed., s.v. "adoption," http://www.biblestudy-tools.com/dictionaries/eastons-bible-dictionary/adoption.html.

Now God has us where he wants us, with all the time in this world and the next to shower grace and kindness upon us in Christ Jesus. Saving is all his idea, and all his work. All we do is trust him enough to let him do it. It's God's gift from start to finish! We don't play the major role. If we did, we'd probably go around bragging that we'd done the whole thing! No, we neither make nor save ourselves. God does both the making and saving. He creates each of us by Christ Jesus to join him in the work he does, the good work he has gotten ready for us to do, work we had better be doing. (Eph. 2:8-9 *The Message*)

Understanding the connection between this biblical premise and physical adoption is key to understanding your identity as an adopted child and as an adopted child of God.

This book was written from the perspective of an adopted child who desires to let adopted children — and the parents raising them — know that it is OK you are adopted, and it is going to be OK for you in the future.

My mother and father always told us that God chooses which child to bring into a family —biologically and through adoption — and that God brought us to them to adopt. Having my parents talk about adoption in these terms never made me feel like I had to live up to something. They made it clear that their love was unconditional. I realized also that my adoption was part of God's plan.

The truth is that you are in the family you're in because God chose your adoptive parents to carry out His specific plan for your life. In this way, you were chosen unconditionally to be adopted. The same thing happened when God chose all of us to be adopted into His family through salvation. We had nothing to do with it; the plan was always God's plan. The same is true for your adoption. We have to understand that God chose to adopt all of us when He sent Jesus to die for our sins while we were still sinners. He knew that your life — regardless of how it began — was not an accident; that it had purpose; and that He had a plan to work out your life for His glory.

Although it is God's plan, part of the plan is up to you. Your part is to accept that your adoption is part of His plan, to believe that He has the best plans for you, and to do what you need to do to find your purpose. Most of all, you must passionately refuse to accept anything less for your life.

CHAPTER 1
THE UNITED NATIONS OF ADOPTION

I was born in 1972 in a suburb of Detroit, Michigan, called Mount Clemens. I was adopted at the age of three months. My biological mother was fourteen, and my biological father was eighteen. Like many adopted children, my biological parents were not married and not in a position to raise a child.

My biological mom was in ninth grade and was described as showing little interest in school. There was no history of extended education in my biological family. Neither of my biological mom's parents had gone beyond eleventh grade. My biological father had dropped out of school in the eleventh grade as well. No further information is known about his side of the family.

I share this information to set the context and to provide the circumstances of my adoption. The bottom line is, like most adopted kids, I was off to a rough start, statistically speaking. Being a child born outside of marriage to a single teenage mother in a major metropolitan area, I had two options: door number one or two. Behind door number one was prison. Behind door number two was death before the age of twenty-five.

I'm not being dramatic. The Bureau of Justice Statistics states that from 1976 to 2005, Black males eighteen to twenty-four years old had the highest homicide victimization rates. In addition, Black males eighteen to twenty-four years old had the highest homicide offending rates. According to information gathered by Morehouse College,[4] one out of every twenty-one Black men could expect to be murdered, a death rate double that of US soldiers in World War II (according to the Justice Department).

Assuming I avoided being murdered, Morehouse statistics also said that 69 percent of Black children in America could not read at grade level in the fourth grade, compared with 29 percent among White children. And only 41 percent of Black men graduate from high school in the United States. I'm not a researcher or statistician (and I know stats can be manipulated to prove a case), but even if these stats are way off, it is a miracle that I survived the circumstances into which I was born.

At a certain point, another option opened up for me: door number three. Enter Colin and Ceila (Cindy) Molzen, my adoptive parents. They are both White and had always wanted children. However, there were some complications to overcome.

My dad's first marriage had lasted about five years, but no children were conceived. Subsequently, before he asked my mom to marry him, he told her that they could not have children. They went to the doctor and found out that my dad had a low sperm count. My mom was fine

---

[4] The Morehouse Male Initiative: Statistics on African-American Males, http://morehousemaleinitiative.com/?page_id=178.

with the possibility of not having biological children, as she had never planned on getting married but rather was thinking she would be a single mother and would adopt children.

Because my dad had been told he could not have children, my parents took no conception precautions, and nine months after they were married, they had my older sister, Dawn. About twenty-two months later, my older brother, Matthew, was born. He had jaundice at birth, and my parents' doctor said a third child might have more severe problems.

This news caused my parents to start researching the adoption process. My parents wanted a big family and decided they had a lot to offer another son or daughter. They desired a baby of any nationality, race, or gender, and they would accept a child with mild disabilities.

My dad, a member of the air force at the time, was stationed at K. I. Sawyer Air Force Base when I was adopted. My parents were unique in that time period, as they were not concerned about the race or gender of the adopted baby. In 1972, out of twenty-two Michigan adoption agencies, 2,430 children were placed into adopted homes. Of those 2,430 children, 335 of them were Black. Of those 335 Black children, 130 were placed in White homes. And in 1972 there was a 39 percent decrease from the previous year in placement of Black children with White families.[5]

My parents felt that a baby of a different race or nationality would be more accepted in the air force because of the exposure to many different cultures. My parents recognized God's hand in taking care of them, as they were the last couple accepted into the required class for the

---

[5] National Survey of Black Children Adopted in 1972, September 18, 1973, Viola W. Bernard Papers, Box 162, Folder 7, Archives and Special Collections, Augustus C. Long Library, Columbia University.

adoption process before home studies began in 1971. Although they had been approached about a private adoption, they decided to go the agency route. They underwent much scrutiny of their life and of their ability to care for a child, and they were required to submit character references.

My dad was reassigned to Malmstrom Air Force Base, Montana, as a missile launch officer the summer of 1973. My adoption paperwork was completed in Montana. According to my parents, at that time Michigan was one of the few states that allowed adoptive parents to leave the state before the adoption paperwork was completed.

Final home studies for my adoption were completed in Montana. My parents already had decided they wanted to adopt again because they didn't want me to grow up feeling alone as the only adopted child. So the final home studies for me were used as the initial studies for my parents' next adoption. This time the adoption process went quickly, and they adopted a beautiful, three-month-old Native American girl from the Crow tribe. My parents named her Mary Elizabeth Morningstar Molzen. As if the curious looks they received while carrying me weren't enough, they had added yet another culture into our family.

The Molzen Clan, as my father deemed our family, raised a few eyebrows when we went to the park or out to eat. My sister and I were obviously different from our mother, father, brother, and sister. I remember very early on that my mom and dad told Mary and me that we were adopted. You may be thinking that they had to tell us for obvious reasons; however, I believe they would have done it had we both looked just like them. (I will get into this issue later in the book.)

My parents instilled in us a great love for them, because they not only told us the truth but also showed us that it is OK to be adopted. They did this in many ways, including helping us understand that we were unconditionally chosen to be in their family as part of God's plan. I believe that the fact that they always stressed this is an important element of our identity. They showed us that being adopted made us special and that family isn't about skin color, blood type, or any other biological trait.

Think about that last statement for a moment. My dad and mom taught us, showed us, and lived their life as if we were their own flesh and blood. Words such as *stepfather*, *half-sister*, and *half-brother* not only were unwelcome in our house but also could be grounds for starting a fight with the Molzens. My parents embraced the true nature of adoption.

In our family, adoption was not a temporary thing. It was never an "until eighteen do we part" scenario for my parents. In fact, they did not stop at two adopted kids. They added two more.

While living in Salt Lake City, Utah, my parents started to hear about families that were fleeing from Southeast Asia because of the war that was tearing their countries apart. They read in a local newspaper about how foster parents were needed to take care of "boat children" from these countries. My dad even set aside some news articles about the topic.

After many months, my parents finally decided to give foster parenting a chance and called Children's Aid Society in Ogden, Utah. The agency said that foster parents for boat children were no longer necessary. Despite this news, my dad continued to chat with a social worker, and the two hit it off, as they had similar first names: Colin and Colleen. My dad mentioned that he had two adopted children, and Colleen became very interested in our family. She started to ask my dad all sorts of questions and eventually asked us whether we were willing to come into the office to talk about another potential adoption.

The questions my dad was asked were not out of the ordinary. However, the urgency in which they were posed piqued his interest. He indicated that, regardless of the child's gender or race, we were interested. In a matter of weeks, we again traveled to Salt Lake City, this time to pick up my ten-day-old sister. We had been trying out new names since we found out we would be getting a baby girl and finally decided on Monica Michelle Molzen.

The social worker placed Monica in my parents' arms, assuring us we didn't have to take her if we felt rushed. From that moment, my parents knew we had to have her. She was a beautiful baby — ten fingers, ten toes, and wriggling all about. It was love at first sight, and the deal was sealed when her eyes connected with ours.

Because I was the oldest of the adopted children, and the only one with extra room space, my parents decided to put Monica's crib in my room. At first I thought this wasn't such a good idea, because I knew how much babies cry. However, I soon got used to jumping from the top bunk to the floor and walking over to Monica's crib. I learned to find her pacifier or bottle and put it back in her mouth while still half asleep. I would stare at her and smile as she went back to sleep. It wasn't until I was older that I realized that one of the reasons I was smiling was that, when I looked at her, I imagined our mom and dad doing the same for me. I also realized that we shared a special connection because we are both Black.

Not long after we adopted Monica, my parents began to think about adopting another child, because Monica was more than six years younger than Mary. Since Native American children were no longer available for adoption by non–Native Americans, my parents decided to look for a child who resembled Mary. They were very purposeful in their pursuit of a South American or Asian child. They knew it was meaningful to me when we adopted Monica because she looked like me, and they wanted to offer the same gift to Mary.

My parents tried to work with several agencies, but delays popped up, and eventually they started the process with the Children's Aid Society of Minnesota. The process was very lengthy because international adoption was not as common as it is today. We later found out that our new brother was born as a result of a Korean and non-Korean union (perhaps a Black serviceman). In many Asian cultures, children who are not solely of that particular culture are treated differently.[6]

On April 24, 1983, my dad flew to Los Angeles to pick up a brand-new Molzen. We named our new brother Luke Won Molzen. Luke, along with one or two other orphans, was being escorted to the United States by an off-duty airline stewardess. The stewardess worked with our adoption agency, the Children's Home Society and Family Services of Saint Paul, Minnesota, transferring adopted babies part time. My parents had decided to use this agency due to their international experience. The airlines did this as a public service at no cost to the adoptive family.

The incoming plane was late, so the escorting stewardess had only a couple of minutes to transfer of Luke to my dad, because she had to run to catch her next flight.

Luke had been abandoned, so we didn't have any background on his biological parents or even his birth date. As a result, my parents decided his birthday would be the day my dad picked him up from the airport (April 24). To further complicate things, we had no historical data regarding Luke's medical history, and we were forced to guess his

---

[6] Kirsty Taylor, "Mixed-Race Koreans Urge Identity Rethink," *The Korea Herald*, December 7, 2011, http://www.koreaherald.com/view.php?ud=20111207000908.

biological age. We did discover that he had a Mongolian spot on his lower back, just like Mary, and that similarity was important to her. With assistance from medical doctors, we were able to determine that he was two years old.

Unfortunately, after an extended sickness, Luke developed rheumatic fever in 1995, which affected his heart. His condition required open-heart surgery in July of 2000. At the age of almost twenty-four, Luke caught the flu, and his heart gave out. We'd had the privilege of having him in our family for twenty-two years.

I had the privilege of speaking at Luke's funeral, where I met some of his friends. The one thing that every single person said was that Luke's smile lit up any room he entered. I can still remember the giant poster board full of pictures of Luke's many different smiles, subtle as they were. To this day I still wear his favorite necklace as a reminder to live each day as if it were my last. When I think of my brother, I cannot help but smile.

To say our family was unique at the time might be a bit of an understatement. We have been called many things. Two of my favorites are the Rainbow Coalition and the United Nations. I'm not sure who originally came up with the name United Nations for our family, but I still lovingly refer to us as such.

Our family represented several major ethnic groups, including European Americans, African Americans, Native Americans, and Korean Americans. Any way you look at it, we had a lot of Americans. Our family is a microcosm of the United States of America — a melting pot of race, culture, and personality. In addition and more importantly, I believe our family reflects God's original design for adoption — a pattern that existed in biblical times, more than two thousand years ago, and a pattern that exists today for all Christians.

My parents have accomplished many things. My dad was a Mustang, an air force–enlisted man who became an officer. My mother was a teacher of both mainstream and special-education students. They would tell you, however, that their greatest accomplishment was raising six successful children.

Our United Nations produced six college-educated children. This accomplishment includes an Air Force Academy graduate, captain, and teacher; a mathematics major and software engineer; a public relations practitioner and entrepreneur; a master's-degree-holding clinical social worker; a paralegal; and a website designer, and budding stage actor.

The following chapters will provide perspective on identity and on what it truly means to be adopted, both spiritually and physically, for adopted children (young and old), for their parents, and for those considering adoption. In addition this book will cover issues associated with interracial adoption, open adoption, and emotional phases versus old-fashioned teen angst. Finally it will provide real-world insight for adoptive parents, including helpful tips, lessons learned, the approach my parents took and why, and a discussion of racism. Most importantly, it will dive into the fact that adoption is God's chosen plan for both the adopted child and the adoptive parent.

An early family portrait: Dad, Mom, Mark (middle left), Mary (middle right), Dawn (front left), and Matthew (front right).

Back row: Dad and Matthew. Front row: Mary, Mark, and Dawn (This photo was by Mom. Dad took 95 percent of the shots.)

Left to right: Mark, Matthew, Dawn, and Mary

Captain Molzen (rear center), Mom (holding Monica), Dawn (middle left), Matthew (middle right), Mary (front left), and Mark (front right)

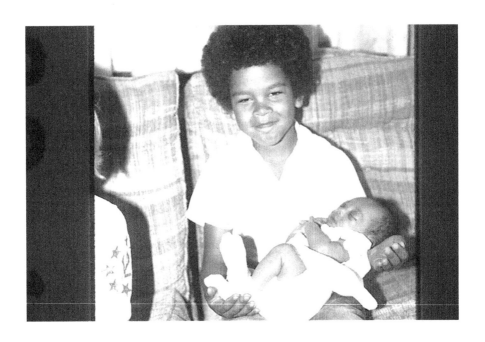

Mark holding his brand-new baby sister, Monica

**Mary (back center with paddle) and Mark, Dawn, and Matthew (left to right) —
a Molzen tradition of birthday paddling**

**The Molzen kids at Christmas. Top row: Dawn and Matthew.
Bottom row: Mary, Luke, Monica, and Mark**

CHAPTER 2
ADOPTED OR CHOSEN? (IT'S TIME TO DECIDE)

There are two types of people in the world: those who see the cup as half full and those who see it as half empty. If you prefer, there are optimists and there are pessimists.

One of my earliest memories of confronting the fact that being adopted meant I didn't know my biological history came after I watched the miniseries *Roots*. This epic show won nine Emmy Awards and shattered Nielsen ratings. It was based on Alex Haley's novel *Roots: The Saga of an American Family*. It had everything to do with family, generations, and tracing your history back to its origins.

As I watched the show, I was spellbound by the story — the struggle to survive and to thrive. My parents had urged me to watch it and tell them what I thought. After I watched it, I felt empty inside. I had just watched a show all about where a family came from — their roots. I don't think this was what my parents expected, but we talked about my biological history and how there were certain things that we would never know. During that conversation, my parents urged me not to dwell on what I didn't have or know but on what I did have and did know. The discussion ended with them telling me that they hoped I knew that I had them as parents for life and that I had their love forever.

I remember feeling like that was good advice, but I still wondered about my past. That was the day I began to look at my past as not something I had lost but as something I could write as I saw fit. Whenever someone said I looked a lot like a professional athlete or I looked like a specific actor, I thought, *Why not?* Maybe I did look like them, because it wasn't out of the realm of possibility that one of them could have been my biological father. This was an innocent daydream that I didn't allow myself to get carried away with.

As you can see, I chose to see my glass as half full. As an adopted child, a parent of an adopted child, or someone considering adoption, you have one choice. That choice will produce a healthy view of adoption for you if you are adopted and a healthy, productive relationship between you and your son or daughter if you are a parent. That choice? Don't play by society's rules or accept their definitions of adoption.

Society still sees adoption as a punch line of sorts. I am sure you have heard someone say that if you act strangely, you must be "adopted." I'm tired of society labeling children created out of wedlock as somehow lower than someone else. I believe we need a fundamental shift in how the adoption community sees adoption, and by making that change, we will begin to influence how society itself sees adoption.

The good news is that this "new" definition isn't mine, and it isn't new. In fact, it's been around for thousands of years. First, adoption is based on being chosen by God, and second, all people are given the chance to accept God's offer of adoption.

To get a true sense of adoption and how that ties into all of our identities — adoptees, adoptive parents, and nonadopted people — I can think of no better place to start than the Bible. I will use a wide variety of translations in this book, all of which reveal the biblical vision of adoption. In addition, the historical church document I studied was the 1646 Westminster Confession of Faith, which outlined how God feels about adoption — the privileges and the process hundreds of years ago.

> All those that are justified, God vouchsafeth, in and for his only Son Jesus Christ, to make partakers of the grace of adoption: by which they are taken into the number, and enjoy the liberties and privileges of the children of God; have his name put upon them; receive the Spirit of adoption; have access to the throne of grace with boldness; are enabled to cry, Abba, Father; are pitied, protected, provided for, and chastened by his as by a father; yet never cast off, but sealed to the day of redemption, and inherit the promises, as heirs of everlasting salvation.

This Confession was written at the time of a great revival called the Reformation, when the church discovered great biblical teachings, including adoption. Both the Bible and the Confession help us see that all who believe in Christ as Savior are adopted — chosen to become brothers and sisters in Christ.

It is my prayer that as you are reading this, you will not be distracted by which Bible translation was or was not used, which denomination this most closely aligns with, or even which theological foundation this book is written on. I believe that God is bigger than denominations, bigger than theological debates, and bigger than any man-made division. I truly believe that there are hurting people — both adopted and nonadopted — who need to understand and accept their God-given identity.

From the very beginning, God chose each of us who would later respond to Him to be adopted into His family. According to Ephesians 1:5, He didn't just plan it; He predestined it:

> Having predestinated us unto the adoption of children by Jesus Christ to himself, according to the good pleasure of his will. (KJV)

God takes pleasure in adoption; it has been and is His plan. In fact, He tells us in Romans 8:23 that we should eagerly await our own adoption. Parents who adopt know that the adoption process doesn't happen overnight, but they eagerly desire it to be. The reality is that physical adoption is a long, detailed, and often complicated process that requires prayer and patience.

I love the description we have in 2 Peter 3:9 (NIV) of the process of accepting the offer of being adopted into God's family. Our adoption shows that the Lord is not slow in keeping His promise, as some understand slowness. The verse states that He is patient with you, not wanting anyone to perish, but everyone to come to repentance. Without repentance, without turning from all our known sin to God, we will never receive the blessing of adoption.

Think about the home studies, references, and paperwork required in the adoption process. We all know that adoptions do not happen overnight. Even after all the studies have been completed and the adoption approved, you never quite know when you will actually get your new son or daughter. All the while, this process requires prayer, petitioning, and, above all, faith.

If you submitted to all of that but kept on practicing some violation of the law, there isn't an adoption agency out there that would give the OK to complete the adoption. God's process requires the same and more for us to be adopted into His family.

The amazing thing about our adoption into God's family is that God did a background check on us. He knew us in our mother's womb, and He already knows our character. He has studied not only what's in our home but also what we do behind closed doors. God's background check revealed all sorts of questionable information, our character references were not credible, and we failed our home study, but God still chose to adopt us into His family. As it says in Romans 5:8, God did this when we truly didn't qualify:

> God demonstrated his own love for us in this: While we were still sinners, Christ died for us. (NIV)

He did this knowing that, despite our best intentions, even our hearts are wicked, as it says in Jeremiah 17:9 (NIV):

> The heart is deceitful above all things and beyond cure. Who can understand it?

The bottom line is that He died for us in order to make our salvation — adoption into his family — possible.

When I talked to my parents about the adoption process, they said it was a long process and that they were never sure when they were going to get the call that a child was available. Although their paperwork had been filled out, reviewed, and approved, the exact timing of my adoption was not known. In fact, the timing didn't really work out well at all. Before my adoption was completed, my father received orders to ship out to his next air force assignment, which was in Montana.

God's timing rarely matches our timing, and His ways rarely match our ways. What was true for my adoption is also true for all our spiritual adoptions. In Galatians 4:4-5, we see evidence of just how different God's timing is from ours:

> But when the fullness of the time was come, God sent forth his Son, made of a woman, made under the law, to redeem them that were under the law, that we might receive the adoption of sons. (KJV)

As a military brat, I learned to tell military time, to interpret the hands of a clock, to read digital clocks, to understand time zones, and even to tackle "world time" (Greenwich mean time, or GMT). However, I've never seen a clock that can tell me when the fullness of time occurs. Of course, that's because God doesn't see time the way we do. He created time but is not subject to time itself. In Ecclesiastes 3:1, we learn that there is an appointed time for everything:

> There is an appointed time for everything. And there is a time for every event under heaven. (NASB)

In other words, although we know God offers adoption, we do not know the timing of the acceptance of that offer. This should be reassuring to those of us who are praying and believing that our children, friends, and other loved ones will receive salvation.

The reality of being adopted into God's family is that, unlike most adoptions, we have an active choice in the decision to become part of God's family. John 1:12 speaks to us as having the power to believe in Christ, to receive Christ, and to become the sons and daughters of God:

But as many as received him, to them gave he power to become the sons of God, even to them that believe on his name. (KJV)

I believe that life comes down to choice. Sometimes it means choosing the lesser of two evils, but I truly believe that you have a choice. After all, God made a pretty tough choice Himself: He chose to give His Son to us as our Savior.

When I became the son of Colin and Cindy Molzen, I received certain rights and opportunities that I did not have before. I was taken out of an environment where the statistics said that I should not have finished high school — let alone college — where I could have been killed, incarcerated, or on drugs. God does the same for all of us, adopted and nonadopted alike. He gives us freedom from our circumstances, releases us from captivity, and places us on a path to a purpose that is beyond our comprehension. In other words, there are immeasurable benefits to being adopted.

Romans 8:15-17 provides great perspective on exactly what it means to choose to be adopted by God — to become a child of God:

> This resurrection life you received from God is not a timid, grave-tending life. It's adventurously expectant, greeting God with a childlike "What's next, Papa?" God's Spirit touches our spirits and confirms who we really are. We know who he is, and we know who we are: Father and children. And we know we are going to get what's coming to us — an unbelievable inheritance! We go through exactly what Christ goes through. If we go through the hard times with him, then we're certainly going to go through the good times with him! (*The Message*)

What an amazing picture this passage paints! It speaks to the fact that when we are adopted, it's a big deal, and we should treat it as such. Being adopted is something to shout about —physically and spiritually. Verse 15 says that it's an adventure to be taken with a childlike attitude of "What's next?" I believe we must choose to greet each day with expectation, not exasperation. Every day and in every moment, we make a choice about how we feel about being adopted. This choice does not ignore our past but looks to the future with faith.

Verse 16 goes on to talk about our identity, something many adopted people struggle with. The good news is that when we are adopted in Christ, the Holy Spirit confirms our identity. This means that if you're struggling with your adopted identity, God answers that question. If you have a great adoption situation, you can choose to accept that God has given you a new identity not only in Him but also in your new family. If you don't have a positive adoption story, you still have a choice to make: choose to accept your identity in Christ. If you haven't accepted Christ as your Lord and Savior, I encourage you to do so right away, because He wants to adopt you and give you a new identity.

God, in His mercy, has given us the way to learn about our new identity by learning about Him. As we read the Bible, pray, and attend Bible studies and discipleship groups, we learn that God's identity is our identity. It is His plan that we become Christlike in our nature.

The amazing thing is that after we're adopted into God's family, there is more — so much more. When you are adopted, it's not as if your parents completed the studies, surveys, and paperwork, and then the job was done. The same is true with God's adoption process. When we become part of His family, we gain an unbelievable inheritance in Christ. We gain access to all the rights and privileges that come with being part of His family. God's generosity doesn't end. He gives us wisdom when we ask, He answers our prayers, He gives us peace, and so much more.

The most amazing thing He does is that He puts His name upon us. We become Christians: followers of Christ. In Jeremiah 14:9, it says that we are called by God's name. In 2 Corinthians 6:18, it goes a step farther:

> And I will be your Father, and you will be my sons and daughters, says the Lord Almighty. (NLT)

This is an amazing picture of adoption. When an adopted child joins a family, the parents are literally (or at least figuratively) saying they will be parents to their child: "I will call you son [or daughter]. You are mine; you are a part of this family; and I love you." I think it's very interesting that adoptive parents write their name onto an adopted child's birth certificate — thereby giving that child their name. In Revelations 3:12, the same type of thing occurs when God says, "I will write upon him my new name."

It is amazing to me that God doesn't stop at just giving us His name; He goes way beyond that. When we are adopted into God's family, He gives us His Spirit, which connects us to Him. When we are physically adopted, at some point we make a decision to accept our adopted family as our own family. If we do not do that, if we choose to remain detached, if we choose to wonder where our "real" family is, then we truly miss out on all that our adopted family has to give. The same is true when we receive the spirit of adoption by accepting salvation. God has gifts to give us, but we have to accept them.

Romans 8:15 paints a picture of one of those gifts (adoption) and the result of receiving that gift: a connection to our Father. This concept is reinforced in Galatians 4:6 when it states that because we are sons, our hearts cry, "Abba, Father." This is not merely us calling out to our Father, but rather it represents a deep, emotional connection.

In Ephesians 3:12 and Romans 5:2, we learn more about other gifts our loving Father God gives. He gives us boldness, confidence, faith, grace, and hope. These are the attributes of adoption and the gifts we receive when we embrace our adoption — both spiritual and physical.

> In whom we have boldness and access with confidence by the faith of Him. (Eph. 3:12 KJV)

> By whom also we have access by faith into this grace wherein we stand, and rejoice in hope of the glory of God. (Rom. 5:2 KJV)

The similarity between how God adopts us and how we are physically adopted doesn't stop at the giving of gifts. The emotional aspect of adoption is reflected in God's approach as well. A loving set of parents often adopts because they have compassion, and they are confident they can give an adopted child a better life and provide a good place to live. The biblical perspective on adoption is expressed in Psalm 103:13 when it speaks of compassion and Proverbs 14:26, which describes God providing confidence and a safe place.

> As a father shows compassion to his children, so the LORD shows compassion to those who fear him. (Ps. 103:13 ESV)

> In the fear of the Lord is strong confidence: and his children shall have a place of refuge. (Prov. 14:26 KJV)

God has described the love He has for us as His adopted children in Matthew 6:30 and 1 Peter 5:7. I truly believe this is the love our adoptive parents wish to give us, if we choose to accept it. This is much like God's approach; He will not force His love on you and neither will your adoptive parents. I often think back on just how loving, patient, and kind my parents were, and I see the biblical pattern that God gives to all who receive salvation and become His adopted sons and daughters.

In Matthew 6:30-33, God speaks to the value He places on all His children and the beauty He sees in us. Verse 30 uses a simple example to remind us that God knows our needs, cares about them, and provides for them as a father provides for his child. In 1 Peter 5:7, the verse addresses the worry we have that our needs will not be met. Whether your adoptive parents meet your needs or not, God's original pattern of adoption was for parents to meet the needs of a child. In Christ we have confidence that He will never let us down in this area.

> If God gives such attention to the appearance of wildflowers — most of which are never even seen — don't you think he'll attend to you, take pride in you, do his best for you? What I'm trying to do here is to get you to relax, to not be so preoccupied with getting, so you can respond to God's giving. People who don't know God and the way he works fuss over these things, but you know both God and how he works. Steep your life in God-reality, God-initiative, God-provisions. Don't worry about missing out. You'll find all your everyday human concerns will be met. (Matt. 6:30-33 *The Message*)

I love how *The Message* paraphrase brings perspective to "God-reality," "God-initiative," and "God-provisions." Your adoption experience may not have included a loving father, a providing father, or one who instilled the initiative to succeed. However, as an adopted son or daughter of God, you do have access to these things. I'm not trying to minimize bad experiences, such as parents who made horrible choices or things that were forced on you. However, consider Revelation 21:5:

He that sat upon the throne said, Behold, I make all things new. (KJV)

That means that God can and will provide these things for you as His adopted son or daughter.

God has prepared good and great things for you if you choose to accept His adoption and to become part of His family. When you choose to lay down your cares, disappointments, and personal desires, God opens up His plans for you — the special plans reserved only for His children. These are plans that no eye has seen, no ear has heard, and no mind has conceived, as it says in 1 Corinthians 2:9.

When you make the choice to accept and to embrace the fact that you are adopted as part of God's plan for your life — that you have been chosen unconditionally to be adopted — that means you're all-in. When it comes to identity, it's all about having a good attitude. After I made the conscious choice to accept my "adopted identity," I felt like a weight had been lifted off of me. When I was headed to an amusement park with *my* family, going out to the movies, or during a birthday celebration, I remember thinking how great it was to be adopted. I had hope for the future, and I felt I could move forward rather than focus on a past that had nothing to do with me or anything I did personally. The best way I know to describe this is found in Proverbs 13:22:

Hope deferred makes the heart sick, But when dreams come true, there is life and joy. (NLT)

The choice I made not only destroyed walls I had built up between me and my parents but also was a step toward God's plans for me. Of course, most Christians are familiar with Jeremiah 29:11, which talks about plans:

For I know the plans I have for you," declares the Lord, "plans to prosper you and not to harm you, plans to give you hope and a future. (NIV)

However, I truly started to feel and now know that my adoption was not an accident, as it says in Psalms 139:16:

Every day of my life was recorded in your book. Every moment was laid out before a single day passed. (NLT)

As I said, I chose to be all-in. This means that not only my adoption but also adoption itself is part of God's plan. Either we, as Christians, believe that God has laid out every day of our lives or we don't. I refuse to believe that God "lost" a few days of my life, that He wasn't aware that I had been conceived, or that I happened to end up adopted. God is mighty, sovereign, and righteous.

I may not understand everything that has happened to me or why, but I do understand that God loves me, He loves you, and He is for me and for you. He is not against us. I decided long ago that figuring out the reason why certain things happened to me would mean that I didn't need faith. That is not a good thing because God says that without faith it's impossible to please Him. Personally, I don't want to go through life without faith. How about you?

My thoughts of adoption weren't always so great when I was being disciplined. When I had done something wrong and was waiting to receive my punishment, I thought that my biological parents would have probably let me go without a spanking. One time, I did something that caused my mom to utter the words that no child ever wants to hear: "Wait until your father gets home." I sat on the edge of my bed, waiting for Dad and wondering what horrible punishment awaited me. Somewhere along the way, I decided that I was probably getting a spanking, and if I put some magazines in my pants, it wouldn't hurt as much. I have a tip for any kids reading this and thinking that was a good idea: don't do it. My dad figured out what I was doing (the square butt gave me away), and a swat or two was added for my attempt.

It would have been easy to use my punishment, and my failed attempt to avoid punishment, as one more reason why my adoptive parents weren't my "real" parents. However, when I accepted that I was adopted and remembered that I was chosen unconditionally to be in this family, I decided to let it go.

Many years later I discovered that God Himself disciplines His adopted children. In fact, He describes it as loving His children. The key in His discipline, and hopefully the discipline you receive or you give, is love, not anger. His intent is never to make your life harder through discipline.

> For the Lord disciplines those he loves, and he punishes each one he accepts as his child. (Heb. 12:6 NLT)

Why? Because the Master won't ever walk out and fail to return. If he works severely, he also works tenderly. His stockpiles of loyal love are immense. He takes no pleasure in making life hard, in throwing roadblocks in the way. (Lam. 3:31 *The Message*)

I know that the adoption process isn't perfect. Some of you reading this book may have been adopted more than once or spent years in the foster care system, waiting. I cannot say that every adoption here on earth is perfect; we live in a fallen world. However, I *can* say that God's adoption process is perfect. He offers, and we choose to accept; He gives gifts, and we choose to receive them; He disciplines us, and we mature.

At the end of the day, we all must make a choice to accept God's adoption perspective. We must choose to accept the truth that we are chosen — adopted — once or twice (here on earth and by our Father in heaven). Know this: God will never abandon you. God adopts for life.

The real issue isn't whether we who believe in Christ are all adopted — we are. Rather, the real issue is whether we will make a choice to accept all that God has to offer. The same is true for our adoptive parents. We have to decide to accept God as our father, and we have to decide to accept our parents as our parents. That means we aren't looking for a better deal, wondering what's missing in our lives or wavering in our decision.

The Bible talks about this type of approach, how it saddens God and how it's not acceptable to Him. I had read James 1:7-8 many times and knew the verse spoke about being double-minded, or indecisive. I never had considered that, by not accepting my adopted identity, I was being double-minded. As a result of this approach, I felt empty. I certainly wasn't receiving anything from God, because I had not accepted that adoption was His plan for me. As a parent I now read this verse and realize that when I have planned to bless my children, and they can't see it or won't accept it, it truly saddens me. I believe God is no different.

When I read Ephesians 4:30 and James 1:7-8, I began to look at them differently in the context of how I had treated my parents at certain times and how for a short time I thought I was incomplete because I didn't know my "real" parents. I spent so much time being angry, emotional, and detached, even though I had loving parents right in front of me who wanted to give me all that I needed. The truth of the matter is that I was struggling with feeling rejected by my biological parents and struggling with my adopted identity, my identity as a Molzen. In spite of my issues, my parents continued to love me through those moments.

> And do not grieve the Holy Spirit of God [do not offend or vex or sadden Him], by Whom you were sealed (marked, branded as God's own, secured) for the day of redemption (of final deliverance through Christ from evil and the consequences of sin). (Eph. 4:30 Amplified Bible)

> Such people should not expect to receive anything from the Lord. Their loyalty is divided between God and the world, and they are unstable in everything they do. (James 1:7-8 NLT)

The reality of spiritual and physical adoption is that it is a choice to accept either one.

Along the way, there are ups and downs, and there are good attitudes and bad.

In order that you may not grow disinterested and become [spiritual] sluggards, but imitators, behaving as do those who through faith (by their leaning of the entire personality on God in Christ in absolute trust and confidence in His power, wisdom, and goodness) and by practice of patient endurance and waiting are [now] inheriting the promises. (Heb. 6:12 Amplified Bible)

God chose to give us the grace to push through the ups and the downs in order to receive all that He has to offer. He did this so that we would receive all that our adoptive parents have to offer as well.

My father-in-law once said that love is a choice you make each and every day; it is not an emotion. A marriage lasts because two people choose to love each other. I believe that your perspective on what it means to be adopted is a choice you have to make each day. Are you "just" adopted, or have you chosen to accept that your adoption is part of God's plan for your life and that you were unconditionally chosen?

CHAPTER 3
ADOPTION AND RACE

One hot summer in Utah, my mom asked me to go out and weed around our weeping willow trees. I grabbed some ice water, some gloves, and my mom's gardening tool. I remember looking at the trees and thinking how beautiful they were. As I finished weeding, a little White girl and her mom walked in front of where I was weeding. I looked up at the little girl, who was five or six years old, and smiled as she slowly walked along. Her mom began to pull her arm as the little girl looked at me with a quizzical expression.

Time and time again, the mom yanked her daughter's arm as the girl looked my way. Just as they walked off our property, I heard the little girl say, "Mommy, look at the chocolate man." This earned her one more quick yank of the arm and an embarrassed look from her mom. This wasn't when I realized that I was different from most people in Utah, but it certainly sums up some of the issues that race presents.

The issue of adoption and race has created a debate that I believe will rage until the end of time. The key issues revolve around whether or not a parent can provide a culturally sensitive environment for a child who is not of their race. In other words, should a White family adopt a Black baby, a Hispanic baby, an Asian baby, a Native American baby, or any race other than its own?

The majority of adoptions today are not transracial (involving two or more races). This means the majority of children within public and private adoption agencies that are African American or Black, Hispanic, mixed race, or in the foster care system are not being adopted. Adoption of Native Americans by non–Native Americans is controlled by the Federal Indian Child Welfare Act, making this type of adoption difficult.

According to the Adoption and Foster Care Analysis and Reporting System: Department of Health and Human Services report (October 2009), there are more than 423,000 children in US foster care. Of those children, approximately 115,000 of them are available for adoption.

The ratio of available children to adopted children in 2009 — approximately 1:22:1 — is troubling. The average age of a child waiting to be adopted in the foster care system is eight. The problem is that they typically aren't waiting alone. In other words, many of them are separated from siblings during their wait. The younger children, often deemed more adoptable, are the lucky ones, as just shy of thirty thousand children turned eighteen and left the foster care system in 2009. For those who "time out," or turn eighteen, the wait for an adoptive family is over.

Adoption often can be expensive. However, foster care adoption often can be more affordable, because home studies and court fees as well as post-adoption subsidies are included. In addition, thousands of employers offer paid time off for adoption and financial reimbursement, and federal and/or state adoption tax credits are available.

When the need is so great, why are so many children not being adopted? One might say that adoption has fallen out of favor in the attitudes of Americans. However, the Dave Thomas Foundation for Adoption conducted the National Adoption Attitudes Survey and found that 63 percent of Americans hold a favorable view of adoption, and 78 percent think more should be done to encourage adoption. That same study showed that approximately 40 percent of American adults — that's about 81.5 million people — have considered adopting a child. Statistically this means that there shouldn't be any children left out of the adoption process.

So where is the gap in the adoption process? While recent studies are hard to find, and they are hidden by differences in foster care and international studies, the answer is race.

There is an old saying that you should never talk about religion or politics. I would add race to the mix. The reality is that issues of race complicate things. Discussing issues of race…well…that's downright controversial. As I mentioned earlier, 1972 wasn't a particularly good year to be Black and waiting for adoption. In fact, it was that year that the National Association of Black Social Workers took a staunch stand against placing Black children in White homes. Key reasons behind this stand included the belief that the process was artificial and unnecessary.

Despite the fact that dozens of studies show that transracial adoption produces stability (approximately 75 percent adjust well in their adoptive homes), legislation had to be put in place. Two key laws addressed the complicated issue of race and adoption: the Howard M. Metzenbaum Multiethnic Placement Act (MEPA) and the Interethnic Adoption Provisions, an amendment of the MEPA.[7] The purpose of these acts was to prohibit any delay in the adoption of a child based on race, color, or nation of origin.

Studies on transracial adoption are few and far between. A key issue is that the same agencies seldom conduct additional studies. The most widely quoted study on transracial adoption occurred years before legislation came into play. According to a study performed in 1987 by the National Health Interview Survey (NHIS), only 8 percent of all adoptions include parents and children of different races (http://www.cdc.gov/nchs/data/ad/ad181.pdf).

The NHIS study showed that 1 percent of White women adopt Black children. The number increased to 5 percent when you add in other races. The numbers weren't much different looking at it from the other end; only 2 percent of non-White women adopt White children. Simply put, most people do not adopt children who are of a race different from theirs. (These figures do not include foreign-born adoptions.)[8]

In 1998, the US Department of Health and Human Services conducted a study that found that approximately 15 percent of the thirty-six thousand adoptions of foster children were transracial or transcultural

---

[7] Howard M. Metzenbaum Multiethnic Placement Act (MEPA) of 1994 and the Interethnic Adoption Provisions, http://encyclopedia.adoption.com/entry/Multiethnic-Placement-Act-MEPA/233/1.html.

[8] Bureau of Consular Affairs: US State Department, Fiscal Year 2011 Annual Report on Intercountry Adoption, November 2011, adoption.state.gov/content/pdf/fy2011_annual_report.pdf.

adoptions.[9] This is encouraging data, which seems to show that the laws enacted in 1994 have started to change the transracial environment.

I was able to find updated information included in the 2007 National Survey of Adoptive Parents (NSAP). According to the study, the NSAP is unique in that it delves into the adoption experience and takes into consideration the well-being of not only adopted children in the United States but also their families. The study's methodology included phone surveys with adoptive parents of children under the age of eighteen and includes children adopted from foster care, other countries, and other sources.

The 2007 survey revealed that there are nearly 1.8 million adopted children in the United States — approximately 2 percent of all US children.[10] The most interesting revelation of this study, however, is the dramatic increase in the number of transracial adoptions. The report showed a fivefold increase since the 1987 study. Specifically the study noted that 40 percent of adopted children are not of the same race, culture, or ethnicity as either of their adoptive parents. These figures include single-parent households as well.

A major part of the increase of transracial adoption comes from international adoptions. This is an interesting phenomenon to me, because international adoptions are usually more expensive when you factor in visas, travel, and lodging.[11] Domestic adoption, for one reason or

---

[9] Jo Jones, "Who Adopts? Characteristics of Women and Men Who Have Adopted Children," National Center for Health Statistics, data brief no. 12, accessed January 22, 2011, www.cdc.gov/nchs/data/databriefs/db12.htm.

[10] http://www.cdc.gov/nchs/slaits/nsap.htm.

[11] Eliza Newlin Carney, "The Truth about Domestic Adoption," Adoptive Families, http://www.adoptivefamilies.com/articles.php?aid=522.

another, is seen as more complicated and risky, partly because of the perception that the biological mother or father will "show up."

We had one international adoption in our family (from Korea), and there was little chance of a biological parent trying to track down our brother. However, I still remember when a lawyer in Montana contacted my sister. The lawyer informed her that her biological mother had died and left a small estate. The notification also mentioned that she had two biological sisters, which caused us to reach out to my sister's biological sisters. It was an emotionally challenging time for my sister, and there was limited interaction after that point. Each time my sister visited her biological sisters, it was at the request of our dad. She felt no need to connect, since she already had two sisters.

According to the US State Department, intercountry adoption statistics show that more than eleven thousand children became part of US families in 2010. Popular countries included the People's Republic of China, Ethiopia, Russia, South Korea, and Ukraine. Overall, in 2010, 11,059 immigrant visas were issued to children through adoption. These included more than a hundred different countries and all fifty US states.

While this sounds like a large number, international adoptions are actually declining. In 2004, there were almost twenty-three thousand international adoptions. The number has been declining steadily since then. Based on current US State Department figures, the numbers for 2011 international adoptions will be somewhere around ten thousand.[12] There are a number of factors in the reduction, including political unrest, negative publicity, and the economy.

---

[12] Bureau of Consular Affairs: US State Department, Fiscal Year 2011 Annual Report, http://adoption.state.gov/about_us/statistics.php.

Adoption Statistics over the Last Decade (US State Department)

From 2000 to 2008, the average number of international adoptions by US families was much closer to 20,000 a year. In 2000 there were 18,857, and until 2008, that number did not drop below that level. In 2009 there were 12,753 international adoptions.

Transracial and international adoption is a complicated process involving race, culture, and identity. Given that our family included multiple transracial adoptions and one international adoption, I know this to be true. I also know that adopted kids and their parents struggle with how to instill a sense of racial and cultural pride while balancing that with a sense of family when they do not all look the same.

I believe my parents' solution to this complicated issue was unique, loving, biblically correct, and bordering on embarrassing. My dad purposely connected with African American couples and found Native American and Korean American people to befriend. At the time I thought my dad simply liked talking with people. However, hindsight revealed that my mom and dad's desire to make our culture a priority overpowered any concern they might have had about being embarrassed.

Whenever possible, and I mean *whenever*, my parents took our family to events that reinforced pride in our culture. As an African American, I learned about my ancestry, important people, and events in my people's history. My parents taught me about George Washington Carver, Harriet Tubman, Frederick Douglass, Martin Luther King Jr., and Rosa Parks. I can't begin to count how many workshops I attended where I listened to speeches, learned to create African drums, and did all types of other fascinating things. My parents would go out of their way to immerse me in every element, including music, hair care, and food. We would eat everything from greens to grits to black-eyed peas to smothered pork chops.

For my Native American sister, our parents tried to incorporate Native American pride into her name by adding "Morningstar" as one of her middle names. We traveled to powwows around the state, watched tribal dances, ate real buffalo steaks (the best steak I've ever had), and even learned Native American beading techniques. When there was a Native American speaker, we were there. When there was a Native American issue, we were in support.

At one point our dad decided he wanted to build a teepee for my sister. This met with mixed results, as he had a hard time finding space in our backyard for a full-sized, authentic tepee. For the record, she and her husband now have a tepee that they sometimes use for camping. My mom took my Korean brother to Korean language classes and experimented with a wide variety of Korean food. This is how I developed a taste for kimchi.

Now, you may be reading this and asking, "What about real-world issues, such as racism? How did you learn about that?"

I believe that our parents prepared us for racism better than if we had been raised in our respective culture. This statement may shock and even upset some readers. My thought process revolves around the issue of perspective. If I had been raised in an African American family, I would have received an African American perspective on racism. Since White parents raised me, I benefited from hearing about how conversations would change when I walked into the room, how I may be passed over for promotions due to racism, and other real-world examples. I received their perspective, gathered through examples of how they had seen White people discriminate against Black people. The bottom line is that when I experienced racism, people didn't go easy on me because of my adoption into a White family.

I'll never forget the day my dad talked to me about racism. He covered all the bases, providing his own definition of racism. Let's look at how racism is defined today.

Dictionary.com defines racism as "1. a belief or doctrine that inherent differences among the various human races determine cultural or individual achievement, usually involving the idea that one's own race is superior and has the right to rule others. 2. a policy, system of government, etc., based upon or fostering such a doctrine; discrimination. 3. hatred or intolerance of another race or other races."[13]

My dad's description went into greater detail, delving into skin color, people's irrational fear of those who were different, and how some people choose to deal with that fear by putting down that different person. However, the most poignant thing he said to me was how people would not say things about me when I was present, how they would not tell certain jokes, and how I would not even know that's what was being done to me. That was racism — the things that were and weren't done to me, and I didn't even know it. My dad told me of times when people told jokes, only to get red in the face when he called them on it after showing them pictures of his family.

This harsh reality must be shared when you have adopted a child who is not of your own race. By having this type of conversation, your child will be equipped to handle, rather than be shocked by, racism.

---

[13] Dictionary.com, s.v. "racism," http://dictionary.reference.com/browse/racism?s=t.

As I said before, the issue of race will be with us until the end of time. Christians, however, are called to act differently. That is not to say that we ignore the existence of racism and the importance of race and culture. Accepting the fact that we are all adopted into Christ's family allows Christians who adopt to have a different kind of conversation with their adopted children. After all, according to Malachi 2:10, we all have the same Father God. In Matthew 6:9, we call on our Father when we pray, and in Ephesians 4:4-6, the issue is settled as it states that there is but one God and Father of all.

CHAPTER 4
CLOSED VERSUS OPEN ADOPTION

When I was young, I used to think about whether I had biological siblings, and wonder if I had a twin. As I grew older, I realized I did have siblings. Their names were Dawn, Matthew, Mary, Monica, and Luke Molzen. Although my adoption was a closed adoption, when I was about twelve years old, I remember sitting on my bed wondering what it would be like to meet my biological mother or father and what I would say to them. In that moment I realized that I had everything I needed in my adopted family and that the only reason I had to meet my biological parents would be for them and not me. It would be to say thank you for making a loving and amazingly difficult choice. "You did the right thing."

One of the most complicated issues in adoption today is the issue of open or closed adoption. Information about an adoptee's biological past and the parents who gave up a child for adoption is at the heart of the open-versus-closed adoption debate. Information is often protected by law, regulated by the courts, and, in some cases, by adoption agencies themselves.

Confidential court records regarding adoption originally were available not only to those directly involved in an adoption but also to anyone who wanted to search court documents. During the early part of the twentieth century, states started standardizing the registration of births through uniform birth records. Today we know uniform birth records as birth certificates. These too were available publicly to anyone who wanted to conduct a search.

It wasn't until 1917 that any state took action to protect confidential records involved in the adoption process. The state of Minnesota decided to revise an existing adoption law to protect documentation involved in the adoption process.[14] States throughout the country took on this approach in order to remove confidential records from public view. However, this information was still accessible by adopted children and the adults involved in the adoption process.

The confidentiality movement was done in the name of creating adoption standards, bringing about a sense of order, and reducing the stigma of being adopted.[15] Consistent with legal efforts of the time, the idea was to place the welfare of the child front and center. Intended or not, adoption confidentiality created an air of secrecy surrounding the adoption process. Legally it meant that when adoptions were finalized in court, states produced new birth certificates. These new birth certificates listed the adoptive parents and sealed the original with the court. Original birth certificates listed the names of biological parents, or at least the biological mother.

---

[14] Minnesota Adoption Law, 1917. http://pages.uoregon.edu/adoption/archive/MNadoptionlaw.htm

[15] "U.S. Children's Bureau, 'The Confidential Nature of Birth Records,' 1949," The Adoption History Project, http://darkwing.uoregon.edu/~adoption/archive/UscbTCNOBR.htm.

This atmosphere of secrecy was fueled by the stigma associated with infertility and children born out of wedlock. It was encouraged by embarrassed parents and relatives, and it enabled adoptive parents to avoid telling their children that they were adopted at all. After World War II, there was an increase in births to unwed mothers, which further fueled a secretive approach.

This mind-set produced maternity homes staffed mostly by Christians. Although these homes are considered controversial by some because they played into the social mind-set of "hiding" unwed mothers, their purpose was to reflect God's love for the lost and fallen. In fact, the Florence Crittenton Mission's original charter was to create a safe haven for "lost and fallen" women. Florence was the wife of a wealthy New Yorker, and the Crittenton homes were formed when Charles Crittenton crossed the United States, donating five hundred dollars to any town willing to start a maternity home.

Maternity homes were not the only reflection of the ideals of the time surrounding adoption. The common adoption approach of matching (see appendix B) benefited from the production of new birth certificates. A new birth certificate, which did not list the biological parents' information, furthered the illusion of adopted children being biological children.

After World War II, there was a significant shift in the open-versus-closed adoption landscape. Confidentiality evolved into secrecy, which meant all records for all parties involved became sealed upon the finalization of the adoption.[16] This prevented any insight into an adopted child's birth or background. While I do not believe this was malicious, it

---

[16] "Child Welfare League of America, 'Proposal for Analysis of the Sealed Adoption Record Issue,' 1973," The Adoption History Project, http://pages.uoregon.edu/adoption/archive/CwlaPFAOTSARI.htm.

did hurt adoption's image, because people were used to open adoptions and questioned the change. As with most changes in life, people resisted and questioned this change.

Fueled by distain for sealed records, the Adoptees' Liberty Movement Association (ALMA) was formed in 1971. They believe that the denial of an adult human being's right to the truth of his origin creates a scar in his soul. They, along with other antisealed-records organizations, have brought the closed-versus-open adoption discussion out into the open. Their key efforts are focused on adoption search and reunion.

Although there have been many legal attempts to change closed adoptions, there have been few victories. The most notable was achieved in Oregon in 1998 when Ballot Measure 58 was passed, which stated that any adopted person twenty-one and older, born in the state of Oregon, was to be issued a certified copy of his or her unaltered, original, and unamended certificate of birth.

My birth certificate contained my adoptive parents' information and nothing to link me to my biological birth parents. I am a strong believer that no one can live in two worlds — the past and the present. I believe my adoptive parents represented my present and therefore future world, and my biological parents represented my past.

Many people say that closed adoptions are secretive. As a public relations person, I look at this as perception versus reality. Given technology today, the Internet, and changes in laws, I truly believe that I could find my biological mother, or at least her family. But I am grateful that my records are sealed. I do not live in the past, and I believe accepting that you are adopted is significantly harder if you are still in contact with your biological parents. In my opinion, if biological parents want to remain involved, they are being double-minded by not fully committing to the choice and by not allowing an adopted child to fully connect with their adoptive parents. That said, I know that open adoptions, with committed parents on both sides, can and do work.

My opinion is not a popular one. However, I do believe it is a biblical one. James 1:8 speaks of being double-minded and warns the reader to expect nothing with this mind-set. Philippians 4:11 talks about learning to be content in your situation. And Psalms 100:3-5 reminds us that God created us, that He is good, and that His love endures forever. I truly believe adoption is God's plan and pattern and that Jeremiah 29:11 is not a Christian cliché but rather the explanation that my adoption and your adoption is not a mistake.

Given that closed-versus-open adoption is an issue so charged with emotion, there have been several attempts to create a compromise in this area. According to a 2009 study done by the US Department of Health and Human Services, nearly all states seal adoption records after an adoption is finalized. However, most states do allow those involved in the adoption process to gain access to nonidentifying information from an adoption record.[17] The overall goal is still to protect the interests of all involved.

Nonidentifying information is usually listed in an adoption file. This file includes details and descriptions surrounding an adopted child's biological relatives and is generally given to adoptive parents. My parents gave me my file when I turned eighteen. In it, and in most files like this, is information on the date and place of my birth, the age of my biological parents, and a physical description of them, which includes eye color, hair color, height, and build. In addition, the file includes my race, ethnic

---

[17] US Department of Health and Human Services, Child Welfare Information Gateway, 2012, http://www.childwelfare.gov/systemwide/laws_policies/statutes/infoaccessap.cfm.

makeup, religion, and medical history of my biological parents. The final portion of nonidentifying information in my file is what grade my biological mother and father completed, their occupation at the time, the reason for placing me up for adoption, and notes on whether I had any biological brothers or sisters. This was the information included in my file; other files may include more or less information.

My file answers basic questions about my biological history, and it certainly piqued my curiosity. However, I wasn't curious about the usual things. In my file, included in just one line, was the fact that my biological father was a professional drummer. I remember playing snare drum in high school and the day I had my first opportunity to play a drum set. I sat down and played and then eagerly looked to my peers and the band instructor to see what they thought. The response was unanimous: I was horrible. I thought for sure that, if nothing else, my biological father's skills had been passed along. Years later I even tried out for our church's praise and worship team as a drummer, only to be rejected again. A few years after that, I tried out again and became one of our church's main drummers. I know God has a sense of humor, and I can't say whether I got my drumming skills biologically or that God gave them to me after getting tired of me praying for them.

Many adopted kids want to learn more about their biological history. Once adopted children are eighteen or older, regardless of the state they reside in, they can access nonidentifying information. An adoptive parent can access this information at any time through a written request. Of our fifty states and territories, twenty-eight allow birth parents access to nonidentifying information. This information is limited to the medical and social history of the child. As of 2009, states that allow birth parents access to nonidentifying information include Alabama, Arizona, Arkansas, Colorado, Connecticut, Delaware, Indiana, Louisiana, Maryland,

Massachusetts, Michigan, Mississippi, Montana, New Hampshire, New Mexico, New York, North Carolina, North Dakota, Ohio, Oklahoma, Oregon, Rhode Island, South Carolina, Tennessee, Utah, Vermont, Washington, and West Virginia.

Above and beyond those twenty-eight states, fifteen states also allow access to nonidentifying information to adult birth siblings. This means an adult sibling can find out nonidentifying medical information about an adopted sibling. Those states include Arizona, Colorado, Indiana, Michigan, Mississippi, Montana, New Mexico, New York, North Carolina, Ohio, Oklahoma, Rhode Island, Tennessee, Utah, and Vermont. One thing to keep in mind is that policies and laws are subject to change, amendment, and replacement. For a current list, visit the US Department of Health and Human Services website (www.hhs.gov).

The biggest area of contention in the closed-versus-open adoption debate surrounds access to identifying information. As you might guess, identifying information generally leads to the positive identification of birth parents or of the adoptee. There are many forms of identifying information, including current and past names, addresses, and similar types of information. Nearly all states release identifying information with consent. This consent must be obtained from the person who is being sought, not the person who is searching.

The entire process becomes very complicated if the person being sought has not consented to the release of his or her information. If an adopted child is searching for his or her biological parent, that parent must have consented to the release of information for it to be provided. The release of information under this scenario would require a court order along with a compelling reason to release the information. Reasons might include a serious medical condition requiring access to specific medical records. In other words, the need for disclosure must outweigh the need for maintaining confidentiality.

Thirty-six states allow biological siblings of adopted children to obtain information. This is allowed only after all parties mutually consent. To the displeasure of open-adoption advocates, multiple states have additional restrictions surrounding the release of identifying information.

The restrictions to identifying information are not sinister in nature. States such as Arkansas, Mississippi, South Carolina, and Texas require counseling prior to the release of the information. The purpose of the counseling sessions is to discuss the possible emotional consequences of gaining access to the information and to safeguard the privacy of all involved.

The most compelling compromise, to date, is the mutual consent registry. This is a method used by many states to ensure mutual consent to the release of identifying information. The registries generally involve those directly involved in the adoption process and create an environment where both sides can express a willingness or unwillingness to disclose information. Today thirty states offer some form of a mutual consent registry: Arizona, Arkansas, Colorado, Delaware, Florida, Georgia, Hawaii, Idaho, Illinois, Indiana, Iowa, Louisiana, Maine, Maryland, Michigan, Missouri, Nevada, New Hampshire, New York, Ohio, Oklahoma, Oregon, Rhode Island, South Carolina, South Dakota, Tennessee, Texas, Utah, Vermont, and West Virginia.

Although each state varies on how its mutual registry operates, the general process requires consent of at least one biological parent and the adopted person. The adopted person must be over the age of eighteen; in some states you need to be twenty-one. In addition, some states allow adoptive parents, if the adopted person is a minor, to register for the release of information. To ensure proper consent, the majority of states that participate require affidavits (a written and sworn statement of fact voluntarily made under an oath). A handful of states will release information from the registry as long as both parties are registered and there are no legal reasons not to do so.

States that do not participate in mutual registries do offer alternative methods for finding identifying information. These methods are commonly called search-and-consent procedures, and they authorize a public or private agency to assist a party in locating biological family members. They act as a type of intermediary between an adopted person and a biological parent or relative. The release of information usually requires an affidavit for consent of release for all involved parties.

Although these approaches provide logical compromises, there are pro–open adoption organizations that want even more done in this area. The Child Welfare League of America does not believe that mutual consent registries, or any of the other methods, go far enough. They are pushing for all states to take on the open-adoption records stance that Alaska, Hawaii, Kansas, and Tennessee have taken. On the other side of the argument, the National Council for Adoption believes that protection of the confidentiality of all parties involved must be taken into consideration when regarding mutual registries. There are other groups who feel that mutual registries go too far down the road of invasion of privacy.

I have had many conversations — both growing up and as an adult — with my parents regarding my closed adoption. In particular, my dad has asked me on several occasions whether I have any desire to find my biological parents. The most recent occasion was on my last trip home to visit my parents.

I do not have a desire to seek out my biological parents. I say biological, and not "real parents," as many are prone to do, because I do not feel that my life has been short-changed or is missing anything because I was not raised by my biological parents.

There are many reasons for this perspective, but here is just one: the definition of *parent*. The following includes nine definitions from Dictionary.com.

> parent
>
> *noun*
> 1. a father or a mother.
> 2. an ancestor, precursor, or progenitor.
> 3. a source, origin, or cause.
> 4. a protector or guardian.
> 5. *Biology*. any organism that produces or generates another.
> 6. *Physics*. the first nuclide in a radioactive series.
>
> *adjective*
> 7. being the original source: *a parent organization*.
> 8. *Biology*. pertaining to an organism, cell, or complex molecular structure that generates or produces another: *parent cell; parent DNA*.
>
> *verb (used with object)*
> 9. to be or act as parent of: *to parent children with both love and discipline*.[18]

I find it interesting that out of nine entries or definitions only one — "a source, origin, or cause" — has any direct correlation to a parent

---

[18] Dictionary.com, s.v. "parent," http://dictionary.reference.com/browse/parent?s=t. Emphasis in original.

actually birthing the child. One of the key issues I presented at the beginning of this book is society's definition of adoption. I feel that the people who raised me are my real parents; they are my father and mother, protectors, guardians, and the ones who parented me with both love and discipline. I would challenge you as an adopted child to ask yourself the following questions, which are based on the definition of a parent:

- Do my adoptive parents fill the role of a father and a mother? Yes / No

- Do/Have my adoptive parents serve(d) as my protectors or guardians? Yes / No

- Does *not* sharing the same DNA negate my adoptive parents' love? Yes / No

- Do my adoptive parents discipline me? Yes / No

- Do my adoptive parents love me? Yes / No

- Do parents discipline those whom they love? Yes / No

- Did my adoptive parents adopt me because they love me? Yes / No

If you answered these questions truthfully, then you see that your adoptive parents are in fact your "real" parents. Don't get mad at me; call Dictionary.com.

So, if you do in fact have your real parents, who are in fact your adoptive parents, why the desire to find your "other" parents?

It is natural to desire to see where you came from, find out whether you have siblings, and to see what your relatives look like. However, this becomes unhealthy when you start to believe you are somehow not complete as a person because that part of your life remains a mystery. Your identity — who you are, what you believe in, and how you live your life — is not a function of DNA but rather comes from the family into which you are adopted. Remember, as an adopted child, you gain all the rights, privileges, and identity of your new family.

When God adopts all of us, He confirms who we really are. We know who He is, and we know who we are: Father and children. And we know we are going to get what is coming to us: an unbelievable inheritance (Rom. 15-17). The same is true regarding physical adoption.

I have found that living your life half-in and half-out is no way to live. I chose, and I encourage you to choose, to take an all-or-nothing attitude with your adoptive parents and your identity. Living as if your current life isn't real really isn't living. When you aren't fully committed, you are tentative, indecisive, and not living life to the fullest.

When God adopted us all into His family, He did so through the choice He made to send His one and only Son. The life God wants you to have is not one of regret, one of questioning, or one of sorrow. John 10:10 says, "Jesus came so that we can have real and eternal life, more and better life than we ever dreamed of" (*The Message*). In John 16:33, Jesus said, "Here on earth you will have many trials and sorrows. But take heart, because I have overcome the world" (NLT).

If you live your life threatening to go live with your "real" parents, then you not only hurt your adoptive parents but you also hurt yourself. If you continue to put up a wall between your heart and your parents, you will always feel empty. This approach actually makes a void where there should not be one. That void is perfectly filled by God and your parents —if you will let it be filled.

I am in no way trying to discount the feelings of adopted children or adults who feels connecting with their biological parents will help them complete their identity. As I stated before, I too have had those thoughts and have spent time questioning my identity (even refusing to accept my adoptive family's identity). As you know, adoption can be an emotionally complicated thing that leaves many unanswered questions and creates uncertainty.

Here is one thing of which I am certain, however. Every person in your life will let you down. I would like to say that I have been the perfect son, brother, husband, and father. However, I have let people down and will probably do so again. I'm sure adoptive parents have or will let you down, and you may even feel that your biological parents did the same.

I say all this to assure you that your biological parents will not complete your identity. God is the only one who will not let you down, and only He can define you. Only God can give you your complete identity in Christ. After all, He created you, chose you, adopted you, and gave you the right to become His son or daughter (Rom. 8:15). The choice to go all-in is yours.

CHAPTER 5
PARENTING AN ADOPTED CHILD

can still remember the day I made a phone call that my parents probably never expected. I was about twenty-five years old, and I had never been so nervous about a call to my parents as I was that day. As I dialed the phone, I rehearsed what I was going to say. When they answered, I asked if they were busy and then asked them to sit down. In hindsight, I think I scared them more with the setup than the actual delivery.

That was the day that I called to thank my parents for putting up with me, not killing me, nor disowning me. I had put my parents through a lot. I had talked back to them — a lot —had run away from home, and had gotten my then-girlfriend pregnant at age nineteen. In other words, I was a handful. In addition to thanking them, I asked them to forgive me for what I had put them through. I was able to do this only after I had rededicated my life to God.

Parenting any child can be quite challenging. Guiding a child through the terrible twos, preteen years, teen years, and early adulthood does have its ups and downs. Throwing in the issue of adoption is often like throwing gas on an open flame; things tend to heat up a bit. The issue of identity and adoption creates a special twist to the teenage years. Not only are you dealing with the "usual" teen angst but you also may face identity issues due to adoption.

One of the best things my parents did was to tell me, as soon as I was able to comprehend the topic, that I was adopted. Now you may be saying, "You were Black, and your parents weren't. They *had* to tell you." Technically, yes; they did have to tell me. However, they didn't have to tell me as early as they did.

Starting the discussion as early as possible is a key element to affecting your child's attitude about being adopted. If you take the time to shape your child's understanding, you can have a positive impact on his or her identity from the start. *Adopted* goes from meaning "unwanted" to "chosen" when you share the biblical pattern that we all are adopted.

Children have enough on their mind regarding their identity. The teen years are a season of extreme change. Finding out at that point that they are adopted is not something any child should go through. There are potentially severe repercussions for withholding this information, unless they actually were adopted during their teen years.

In general your child's attitude about adoption is going to be a reflection of your attitude about adoption. In other words, if you don't have open discussions about it, your child can draw the conclusion that being adopted is a dirty secret. In addition, the very words you use will affect your child's perception about why he or she was put up for adoption.

Discussing the why in an age-appropriate way with your child is just as important as discussing the what. You can spend a great deal of time talking about what adoption is, but if you leave out the why, your child will draw his or her own conclusion. In this instance the old adage "No news is good news" is not the approach to take. Explaining why a child was put up for adoption is a sensitive but important subject.

My parents' approach to explaining why my biological mother put me up for adoption made logical, financial, and emotional sense. They told me that my mother was fourteen years old. They explained that my parents weren't together, and my mother hadn't finished school. Finally they talked about my biological mother's emotional choice. She put me up for adoption because she loved me. Now, I could have chosen not to accept this description, but I made a conscious decision at that time to do so.

When my parents appealed to my logic, it wasn't some long, drawn-out explanation. They told me that my mother was fourteen years old, and that was very young. I thought of the fourteen-year-olds I knew. I considered what an average fourteen-year-old was doing — it wasn't having kids. Now you may be thinking, *My child's biological mother was older; how does this help me?* Appealing to a child's logic is about painting a picture from his or her point of view. If your child is ten, then the point of view is ten. If your child is fifteen, then it is fifteen.

When my parents told me that my biological parents were not together, and my mother hadn't finished school, I knew that meant she didn't have much money — what fourteen-year-old does? My parents spent a great deal of time shaping my attitude about college and career. In other words, a college education and a career meant financial stability. My point of reference, and hence my attitude, had already been determined. My parents gave me examples, such as buying groceries, clothes, and toys. This demonstration built on the logical explanation my parents already had provided.

My parents also appealed to my ability to choose to love. The greatest choice is to choose to love! My parents' attitude was that the decision to give me up for adoption was made because of my biological mother's choice to love me. Society would counter that the decision was made in spite of love or that my biological mother had no choice at all. Unfortunately many people your child will come in contact with believe that adoption is an option taken when love is absent. Earlier in this book, I spent some time talking about your attitude and the choices you make. The interpretation of this issue will be deeply affected by how you choose to view why you were put up for adoption. My parents' approach focused on love.

There are so many definitions of *love*. Here are a few definitions from *Merriam-Webster Online*: "strong affection for another arising out of kinship or personal ties…attraction based on sexual desire: affection and tenderness felt by lovers…affection based on admiration, benevolence, or common interests…unselfish loyal and benevolent concern for the good of another."[19]

As I consider my parents' explanation of love as the motivating factor for my being put up for adoption, I can see several reasons why that makes sense. *Love*, as you can see above, doesn't have just one definition. Not every definition fits every context. Society would say that the definitions highlighting family and friendship are the norm. However, the third definition — affection based on admiration, benevolence, or common interests — brings up an interesting point.

---

[19] *Merriam-Webster Online*, s.v. "love," http://www.merriam-webster.com/dictionary/love?show=0&t=1375465861.

If someone makes a decision that is mutually beneficial, is that decision no longer considered an act of love? What this issue comes down to is whether you are a negative or a positive person; or, said another way, are you a victim or a victor? Do you choose to find the issue or the solution?

One could look at a decision based on self-interest or mutual benefit, such as adoption, and label it as bad. Even if the decision was purely selfish, however, the child receives all the love, opportunities, and support the biological mother could not provide. Is not the child loved? In other words, is not the end result still a loving family? Is not the final result love?

If you still are not convinced, here are a few questions to answer honestly.

- Is love a choice, not an emotion? Yes / No

- Does love care more for others than for self? Yes / No

- Does love want what it doesn't have? Yes / No

- Does love force itself on others? Yes / No

- Is love always "me first"? Yes / No

- Does love always look for the best? Yes / No

Regardless of how you define love, these questions are valid questions to ask. At the end of the day, parenting any child is tough. There are many exhaustive resources on raising an adopted child. The most crucial thing in raising your adopted children, however, is showing them biblical love.

When it comes to raising children, I think God's ways are undoubtedly the best ways. As I searched for great advice or wisdom to share in this chapter, the Bible's chapter on love came to mind. I've read it many times, but as I read *The Message* translation, I realized that my parents exhibited many of these qualities in their efforts to raise me right.

As you read 1 Corinthians 13:3-7 below (*The Message*), I urge you to consider this as the outline of how to raise an adopted child — or any child, for that matter. After all, as adopted sons and daughters of God, this is the method He uses with us each and every day.

Love never gives up.
Love cares more for others than for self.
Love doesn't want what it doesn't have.
Love doesn't strut,
Doesn't have a swelled head,
Doesn't force itself on others,
Isn't always "me first,"
Doesn't fly off the handle,
Doesn't keep score of the sins of others,
Doesn't revel when others grovel,
Takes pleasure in the flowering of truth,
Puts up with anything,
Trusts God always,
Always looks for the best,
Never looks back,
But keeps going to the end.

The thing that amazes me is how many elements of 1 Corinthians 13 my parents used with me without directly quoting it or mentioning it. As I said before, as a teenager I was a real handful, and yet my parents never gave up. They certainly cared for me more than themselves; they never kept a list of my many sins. They didn't fly off the handle, and I believe they truly had to trust God while raising six children, four of them adopted.

The most impressive thing about God's recipe for raising all of us adopted children is that He always looks for the best in us. I cannot describe or measure the impact of this principle or accurately portray the impact you as an adoptive parent, or an adopted child, can have by making the choice to believe the best. I urge you to believe the best in your child, believe the best in yourself, and believe the best in the biological parents involved in the adoption. Remember, love keeps going to the end.

CHAPTER 6
THE CHOICE IS YOURS

One sunny summer day, I decided to take my family to Disneyland because my wife and I knew our kids would have a great time. As we arrived at the park, I remembered that a good friend of mine had pointed out once that Disney goes to a great deal of trouble to make sure people have a great time. In fact every person, from the cotton candy vendor to the photographer, reinforces the idea that Disneyland is a great place to visit.

Think about that last moment at the park, when you have ridden all the rides you could, stuffed yourself with cotton candy and funnel cakes, and drank that thirty-two-ounce monster soda. As you are preparing to walk out the gates, you suddenly realize you need to use the restroom and can't find one. Instead of trying to find one by memory or reading the map, you ask an employee (the same one that greeted you when you arrived eight hours earlier). Instead of that "I've worked all day; get out of here" attitude, you get a smile as that Disney employee directs you to the restroom. That truly reinforces the idea that Disneyland *is* a great place to visit.

On the day that my wife and I took our three boys to Disneyland, it was not a great place to visit. Nothing had changed: the park wasn't closed, the giant turkey leg vendors were not sold out, and the "It's a Small World" ride was up and running. The Disneyland employees were not having an off day, and they did not have a bad attitude.

The only thing off was the attitudes of our children. No matter how hard we tried, nothing mattered. I even told them that they were going to have a fun day, whether they liked it or not. Our boys chose to see Disneyland as something for babies and not for them. That day the choice to have a bad attitude won out. I'm happy to say that bad attitudes are a rare thing with our boys. However, this proves the point that no matter what you have planned for the day, how far you traveled to get there, or how much money was spent, if someone has the attitude that they're not going to be happy, they won't be.

The attitude we take and the decisions we make are based on one thing: us. The cold, hard reality of life is that everything in this world can be taken away from you — your possessions, your freedom, and even your life. You may be reading this book and feeling like your biological parents were taken from you, that your "freedom" has been taken from you, and that you are "stuck" with your adoptive parents. I know that feeling because I thought that myself when I was a teenager. It took me many years to realize that my circumstances may be beyond my control, but how I react to them (my attitude) is not. My reaction or attitude is something that I and I alone control. It is something that you and you alone control as well.

You can go through your entire life, or a good portion of it, feeling like you are a victim, believing things like, "My parents didn't want me," "These aren't my real parents," and "This isn't really my family." In fact, you can simply exist and tolerate the home you're in, or you can choose to live life in your home to its fullest. Existing means that you just get by, learn to deal with your so-called family, or cope with the situation, but when you're eighteen, you are out of there! I use the word *exist* because that really isn't *living*. If you have ever thought there must be more to life than this, then you are just existing, and existing isn't living. As I said before, Jesus didn't come here so that we could have a mediocre life. He came so that we could have a full life (John 10:10)!

If you don't make a decision to live life to the full — to accept that Jesus paid a price to adopt you, and so did your parents — then when you leave home, nothing more than your mailing address will change. I know this from experience. I ran away from home and away from that "fake" family. I moved in with a friend of mine from high school. I thought I was being responsible because I kept my summer job and still planned on finishing school.

I had changed my address but not my attitude. I was existing with a family that really wasn't my family. I had traded one situation that I thought was bad for one that took me a month to figure out wasn't any better. Don't get me wrong; my friend's family was great. They opened their home to me, fed me, took me places, and talked with me, but they were not my family. After a while I realized they had less of a vested interest in me than my adoptive family.

I decided to look at the facts of my situation and to make a list of what I had gained by moving out and what I had lost. If you've dreamed of a better life, a life free from your adoptive parents, or if you are simply confused about your adoptive family, I encourage you to make a list with two columns. Those columns are "what I gained" and "what I lost."

Here is a sample of what my list included under what I gained by moving out: freedom from my adoptive family's rules, living on my own, going to bed when I want, and bills (unfortunately). Under what I lost, my list included my family's love (although it never left — I did), a viable future (I was making minimum wage), and order in my life. My list included more elements, but this gives you a sense of how to make your own list.

The results of doing this list weren't quite what I thought they'd be. I have a feeling that, if you have been honest, your list turned out a little different than you might have thought. Keep in mind that when I wrote this list, I had not yet accepted Jesus as the Lord and Savior of my life.

I had to go through this list several times in my head before it came out the way you see it above. Whether you are an adopted child, teen, adult, or parent, your emotions change the way you see your situation. You may need to do two or three drafts of your list. I recommend you write it out, leave it for a day or two, and then see if you feel differently about the list.

When I first did the list, my attitude was all wrong. My list showed that I had a bad attitude. Your attitude is the filter through which you live your life and through which you make decisions. Even now, as you are reading this book, there may be a battle in your mind between a good and a bad attitude about what you have just read. Ultimately you must make the decision to see yourself simply as adopted or to see yourself as unconditionally chosen, first by God to receive salvation, and then by your adoptive parents as part of God's plan for your life.

Either your attitude is that God truly is in control and that He has good plans for your life or that He does not. Either you believe that God truly formed you in your biological mother's womb and that He set you apart for His purposes, or you believe that He made a mistake, and that is why you were adopted.

I don't know which translation of the Bible you have been reading, but every translation of the Bible I've ever seen says that God doesn't make mistakes when He adopts us as His children when He offers us salvation. The Bibles I've read say adoption couldn't possibly be a mistake, because God not only predestined it but also called adoption a good and pleasurable thing (Eph. 1:5). God loves adoption so much that He wants it for all humankind (2 Pet. 3:9), and He tells us we should eagerly await our own adoption into His family (Rom. 8:23). If your adoption story isn't a positive one, if your parents weren't the best, then accepting God's adoption can give you what your adoptive parents should have given you.

God went out of His way to adopt you into His family. It wasn't easy to go from heaven to Earth, to be made of a woman, made under the law, so that we might receive the adoption of sons (Gal. 4:4-5). God is amazing in His adoption process. He does home studies; He knows us inside and out; He appoints a time for our adoption; and He requires a great price, which He Himself pays on our behalf. Ultimately He gives us His name much in the same way that our adoptive parents give us their name (2 Cor. 6:18).

The most amazing part of God's adoption plan is that He not only gives us His name but also our identity, if we choose to accept it. At no time does He force His identity or His plan down our throats. Our identity as adopted sons and daughters of Christ is sprinkled throughout the Bible. If you are struggling with your identity, let me show you who God says you are as an adopted child. I urge you to pray and to declare these verses out loud every day.

You are:

- ➤ A child of destiny, not an accident (Jer. 1:5)
- ➤ A divine project, not an abandoned project (Phil. 1:6)
- ➤ A solution, not a problem (Isa. 8:18)
- ➤ A victor, not a victim (1 John 5:4)
- ➤ A winner, not a loser (2 Cor. 2:14)
- ➤ The apple of God's eyes (Deut. 32:10)
- ➤ Fearfully and wonderfully made (Ps. 139:14)
- ➤ Above, not beneath (Deut. 28:13a)
- ➤ The head, not the tail (Deut. 28:13)
- ➤ A blessing, not a burden (Gen. 22:17-18)
- ➤ A success, not a failure (Josh. 1:8)
- ➤ An asset, not a liability (Prov. 31:10-29)
- ➤ Favored, not cursed (Prov. 8:35)
- ➤ Not in a losing battle (Ex. 14:14)
- ➤ Able to hold your peace (Ex. 14:14)
- ➤ Not defeated (Rom. 8:37)
- ➤ Not weak, but strong (Ps. 29:11)
- ➤ Able to do all things through Christ who strengthens you (Phil. 4:13)
- ➤ A child of joy, not sorrow (Isa. 61:3)
- ➤ Set free (John 8:36)
- ➤ Blessed by God's goodness and mercy (Ps. 23:6)

This is the identity that we have as adopted sons and daughters in Christ. If your adoptive parents didn't reinforce this type of identity in you, then God is willing and ready to do it. In fact God tells us to be encouraged — not discouraged — in 1 Samuel 30:6. He tells us in 1 Samuel 17:32–37 not to be intimidated. I believe if we choose to accept our identity as chosen adopted sons and daughters, He will give us an adventurous, full, and exciting life.

The question is, do you want the identity and the life God promises us? If you do, you must accept all that it entails. You must accept that your adoption is part of God's plan for your life and accept that He chose you, once to be adopted into His family and once to be adopted into your family. You must accept that God works out *all* things for those who love Him and are called according to His purpose (Rom. 8:28).

Purpose is a hard thing to define. Many people ask, what is my purpose or what is the purpose of something that happened to me? These questions are a natural product of our desire for everything to make sense. However, we are not called to our own purpose, and we do not get to define our life's purpose. Whether we like it or not, God does that.

Many people who try to define their life's purpose are left empty, unsatisfied, and broken. They chase this purpose or that purpose only to attain it and yet remain unsatisfied. No, we are called according to the purpose God has designed for our lives. Often when we are fulfilling God's purpose, we feel alive and satisfied. When we do the activities God has for us, time stands still; we get lost in the moment or we don't want to stop. However, in the pursuit of God's purpose for our lives, there will be many days and nights filled with things that do not make sense to us. These are the times we must decide to accept God's purpose for our lives by faith.

I believe that, as you make this decision, blessings (God's plans for you, your parents' plans for you, the love of both, and the life you've been searching for) or curses (depression, anger, and confusion) are before you (Deut. 30:19). I pray that it will not take you as long as it took me to make this decision. If you have lived most of your life having not made this type of decision, it is never too late. Christ makes all things new (2 Cor. 5:17).

I pray that you will choose the blessing of becoming an adopted son or daughter of Christ and the blessing of accepting that your adoption was part of God's plan and that you are unconditionally loved. I know, by faith, that when you do, God will do exceedingly and abundantly more for and with you than you could ever ask for, hope, or imagine (Eph. 3:20).

CONCLUSION

There was a moment in college that I will never forget. It was not when I chose my major, when I aced a test, or even when I finished my last class. This was a day like any other, a day that started innocently enough, with friends hanging out in a dorm room.

On that day a star basketball player who lived on our floor came walking in to see what was going on that night. As usual, he was high. I was hanging out with some football players, basketball players, and other friends from the floor. I cannot remember what we were talking about, but I will never forget what happened next.

The basketball player didn't like something I said and started talking tough. He stood up and towered over me. I am five feet eight, and he was at least six feet five. This highly sought-after and often-recruited basketball player was used to getting his way and having people agree with him. He certainly was not used to someone like me doing anything less than going along with whatever he said.

The next thing I knew, I was staring down the barrel of a gun, and the basketball player was telling me he was right and I was wrong. I know it sounds corny, but time seemed to slow down as I looked at that gun.

I knew that I had a decision to make, a choice. I either could apologize and beg for my life, or I could stand there, refuse to apologize, and thereby risk my life. I foolishly made my choice and told the basketball player that I knew two things. First I knew that I was a Christian and that if he pulled that trigger, I was going to heaven. Second I knew that if he pulled that trigger, his basketball career was over, and he was going to jail.

The basketball player scowled at me, said a few four-letter words, and informed me that I was a dead man because he was going back to his room to get his bullets. I would like to say that I stood my ground. The next thing I knew, however, one of my rather large football friends picked me up and threw me over his shoulder and ran out of the dorm.

In that situation, neither of my choices was particularly good. For the record, I was far from being certain of my salvation at that time, and the choice I made was incredibly foolish. God, in His grace, chose to save me from my selfish pride. However, I knew that I had a choice to make.

Choice is an amazing thing. At its root, choice involves choosing — an active thing, having the right or authority to choose and being chosen. All three elements play a role in choice, and all three elements represent what you must do every day as a spiritually and physically adopted son or daughter.

I urge you to actively make the choice to see your adoption as part of God's plan for your life. An active choice is an ongoing choice. As I researched this book, prayed, and talked to people, I came to the realization that in some ways it is easier to believe that spiritual adoption is part of God's plan than it is to believe the same about physical adoption. The reality is that we have an enemy, as it says in John 10:10, that wanted to abort us, and now wants to steal our identity. If he can't keep us from that, he seeks to destroy any chance of us fulfilling our purpose.

In the face of such attacks, remember that you have the right to make a choice, whether your situation is good or bad. God wanted us to get this point so badly that He put it in writing in John 1:12. He said that to all who receive Him and believe in His name, He gave the right to become children of God. You have the authority to make a choice about how you feel about being adopted.

Finally you must accept that you are chosen. God chose your parents to carry out His plan for your life through adoption. Your choice is to accept that plan. Jesus died so that you would have the right to become an adopted son or daughter of God. The only way to access that right — to accept God's chosen identity for you — is by faith.

I pray that you will choose the plan that God has for you so that you may live your life to its fullest.

APPENDIX A
Q&A: WHAT WERE MY PARENTS (COLIN AND CINDY) THINKING?

Q: What was Mark's adoption like?

A: Starting with Mark, we recognized God's hand taking care of us. Colin must have talked about adoption sometime, because someone approached him about adopting a child privately (theirs or someone they knew at K. I. Sawyer Air Force Base in Michigan). We had already decided to go through legal procedures and, at that time, had received papers from Michigan State Social Service. At our first parent adoptive meeting, we learned our application was the last one accepted for that year (1971).

Our social worker was brand-new and was very thorough, but we felt she was slow. After four or five home visits and a doctor's report for Matthew (she felt his speech was slow), we were qualified, as the doctor said Matthew was fine. After many calls to see if our reports were in, we were notified in early November 1972 that there was a baby boy — three months old — available in Mount Clemens, Michigan. We had a long but uneventful trip down, though we did see a bear run across the road. We arrived, met the social worker, answered some questions, and finally got to see Mark for the first time. We got to hold him and to take Mark David Molzen home. He shared a room with Matthew, and Matthew was quite proud.

We had already planned to take a trip to South Dakota for Jody's naturalization ceremony, which was scheduled shortly before Thanksgiving. Colin's brother and his wife had adopted Jody, a beautiful little girl from overseas. After that we had planned on spending Thanksgiving in Iowa. We were able to introduce Mark to many members of our family. It was very exciting! During our trip back home to Michigan, our car rolled over in northern Wisconsin due to a severe snowstorm. All family members were OK, with the exception of Matthew. He suffered a broken collarbone.

The following summer (1973), Colin got orders for missile duty and school. We had not yet completed Mark's adoption, but we planned on completing it in Montana when we were settled. Later on we were told that most states would not have allowed us to leave the state before completing the adoption.

Q: What was the discussion like between you two when you knew I was Black?

A: I had been married once before, but we had not had children. The doctor had told me that I could not have any children. When I asked your mother to marry me, I told her that we could not have any children. She said no sweat; she had always thought she would be a single mother with adopted children. So we entered marriage knowing that our family would be built through adoption. Nine months after we were married, the Lord blessed us with a little girl (Dawn).

Almost two years later, we were blessed with a little boy (Matthew). Matthew had medical problems at birth, so we decided not to have any more biological children. About two years later, we decided we were ready to expand the family.

We discussed the possibilities of what we might be offered and said we would take a child of any racial background and with medical/physical problems. The good Lord blessed us with four adopted children who didn't have medical/physical problems. We knew beforehand that adopting White children would be hard and require a long wait. The same is true for today with adopting White children. We knew the Lord would bring the right child to us and he did — a little Black baby who grew up to become Mark David.

Q: What were you thinking when you adopted Mary, Monica, and Luke?

A: As soon as we got to Montana, we started the process of completing Mark's adoption. During the home visits, we said that we wanted another child, as we did not want Mark to grow up feeling like the only adopted child. The social workers said we could start paperwork, and they would use home visits for Mark's adoption and for our next adoption. Mary's adoption went faster. By March of 1974, Mary Elizabeth Morningstar arrived. She was three months old when we got her.

While we were in England (1975–1978), and again in Maryland, we made some inquires about adoption. However, nothing came of it. We thought that maybe our family was to be four.

We moved to Utah in February of 1980. At some point, I'm not sure when, Colin cut out an article from the newspaper about boat children in Southeast Asia. He put it in his dresser drawer. One day in June or July, he took it out to make a couple of telephone calls for more information. He ended up talking with Coleen Burnham at Children's Aid in Utah. At first, she could not help us, but after first mentioning our names (Coleen and Colin) and our family, she said that maybe they would be interested in working with us.

We went for an interview at Children's Aid in Utah and filled out lots of paperwork and had another interview. Cindy mentioned that we wanted a baby as young as possible because we knew, from past experience, that many habits were already formed by the age of three months. On August 8, I think, we were called to see if we could come in the next day to pick up our baby girl. This was a great surprise and very exciting. Some family friends said we could borrow clothes and some other things from them, as the adoption had happened so quickly that we didn't have time to get many things ready. We had a bed and a few other items. The next day, we brought home Monica Michelle Molzen.

Monica was six and a half years younger than Mary, and we didn't want her growing up alone. We decided that we needed to find one more child for our family. It seemed quite meaningful to Mark to have someone (Monica) that resembled him, so we decided to look to the Orient or South America to find someone who would resemble Mary. Native Americans were no longer available to non–Native American families.

We contacted the Holt adoption agency, but they would not work with us, as we had five children. We contacted other agencies that we found that were working in South America or the Orient, but did not have much luck. While we continued to look, we noticed that the Children's Aid Society of Minnesota put out monthly newsletters and handled children in Korea and a couple of South American countries. We put in an application and inquired about a few children, but there was always some reason they were not available.

One day we received a call that they thought they had a little boy for us in Korea. We were thrilled. He was approximately nine months old. We were told that he had been abandoned on the steps of a government building near an adoption center in Seoul. Given the proximity to an adoption center, his parents would have known that he would come to America.

We started on immigration papers. The process was discouraging. We made many trips to the immigration office in Salt Lake City, only to wait again and again. The papers were taking forever. Everything else was taken care of and had been finalized. We decided to call our congressman to see if he could help. We are not sure if our congressman was of help, but Luke Won finally arrived April 27, 1983.

Luke had a beautiful smile and fit in our family perfectly. He learned English quickly. After six months, we went to court, and he went through the naturalization ceremony. Luke seemed to feel it was important, and he started to refer to himself as "Lukey, American citizen."

Q: Were you scared about what other people might say about our "United Nations"?

A: Scared is not the proper word. We were a little saddened knowing that not all would accept the adoption situation. We have never considered that we should impose our family on anyone. If they asked, we would explain how our family came about and hope that they might change or modify their way of thinking. Being a military family, our acceptance was easier and less problematic than most civilian locations would have offered. In the military, we were integrated in church, at work, living areas, friendships, et cetera. I doubt if you could find a better place to raise a multiracial family than in the military.

Q: What doubts did you have about instilling in me a sense of racial identity?

A: I would think any White parents would have to give much consideration about how they would raise and provide racial identity to their adopted child. At the time we adopted you, there was much dissent by the Black Social Workers of America and other groups advocating that multiracial adoption was not a good policy because the adoptive parent (when White) could not instill racial identity. We strongly believe that children should remain with their biological parents whenever possible and that adoption by Black adoptees would probably be best. However, when a child is not adopted and spends years in foster care, that is not good. The next best thing is a home where he or she can find love, comfort, and safety. We believe that is any home, regardless of the racial background of the adoptive parents.

As you got older, we tried to attend programs on Black history. We did similar things for all of our children. In addition, the military base often had musical groups that were diverse, and we took you there. We pushed education as a way for you and all the kids to be successful. We didn't try to force ourselves on Black families, but Black families were always accepting of us adopting Black children. I think we were all able to have more Black friends because they realized we were accepting of them. We have only met a few Whites that were opposed to our adopting multiracial children. Of course we have gotten many second looks through the years.

I think our family of adopted children has helped many realize we are all children of God. It has probably helped other families to consider multiracial adoption as their avenue to having a family. At one point we even started an adoption club and had others join. Also we joined other clubs when available.

Q: Did you have a plan to address potential prejudice?

A: Not really; just address it when it happened by talking about it in real terms. I guess you could call that our plan.

Q: Did you originally have a plan to add more racially diverse kids, or did it just happen?

A: I would say we did. Cindy believes it is best for children to have a sibling close in age. Dawn and Matthew were somewhat close in age. So when we adopted you, we knew we would be adding one more child or playmate. I do believe we wanted our next adoption to be a racially diverse child, but I am certain that if a White child had been offered, the child would not have been rejected. I do not see how any parent can reject a little baby when they are placed in your arms.

APPENDIX B
CURRENT VERSUS HISTORICAL ADOPTION

As I looked into what the Bible had to say about adoption, I was curious to know how we came to define adoption as we do today. I felt like the best approach was to look at adoption history and to call out key moments in the adoption story. This section is by no means an exhaustive resource on adoption history. Many of the concepts originate from government studies, private research, census data, and Ellen Herman's adoption history timeline. (Herman is a faculty member in the Department of History at the University of Oregon.) I believe this chapter gives an accurate glimpse into how and why adoption began in the United States.

The year 1851 was important in American adoption history. Although it is widely agreed that adoption was happening in America before 1851, in that year Massachusetts passed the first modern adoption law. It was important because it required adoption to be in the best interest of the child and created a legal framework of exactly what that meant. The act was called the 1851 Adoption of Children Act.

In 1854, a minister and early pioneer of social work, Charles Loring Brace, created "orphan trains." Brace was the founder of the New York Children's Aid Society and organized trains running from the East Coast to the Midwest and even into Canada and Mexico. As the orphan train pulled into stations between the East Coast and the Midwest, potential parents would come to choose children to adopt. These trains ran for more than seventy-five years, carrying approximately 250,000 children to waiting adoptive parents. The adoptions at that time often required very little research into the backgrounds of adoptive parents. The program was innovative but controversial.

Many years later, in 1872, the New York State Charities Aid Association was founded. Its purpose was to create a formal approach to child placement. Building on the movement toward formalizing the adoption process, Michigan became the first state to create requirements for adoptive parents. Those requirements included being of good moral character, being financially able to support an adopted child, being able to educate the child, and possessing a suitable home in which to raise the child. These early legal requirements, which were defined by a judge, form the backbone of the adoptive guidelines used today.

In 1909 adoption was discussed at a national level when the White House held a conference on the Care of Dependent Children. The most significant decision that came out of the conference was that poverty could no longer be the sole factor in justifying the removal of a child from a family.

The next twenty years produced adoption agencies similar to those we see today in America and around the globe. Prior to this time, adoption was not as formalized or organized. According to the research I have done, adoption remained tied to religion and philanthropic elements and driven and defined largely by women. According to the University of Oregon's Ellen Herman, who authored the Adoption History Project, four influential women, early pioneers in social work, helped define modern adoption by founding some of adoption's earliest agencies. These include Louise Waterman Wise, who founded the Free Synagogue Child Adoption Committee. She was the wife of Rabbi Steven Wise, who was involved in founding the NAACP and the American Jewish Congress. She founded the Free Synagogue Child Adoption Committee as part of her tireless work to protect children.

Clara Spence founded the Spence Alumnae Society, as adoption was near and dear to her heart; she adopted two children of her own. Florence Walrath founded the Cradle adoption agency as a result of her sister's experience with infertility and out of a desire to dignify adoption and to improve the quality of child care within adoption agencies. Alice Chapin, wife of a well-known New York pediatrician, founded the Alice Chapin Nursery out of concern for infants that were abandoned in hospitals and shelters.

The adoption approach taken by these women went against the grain of that time. Their view of adoption was optimistic rather than pessimistic. The prevailing attitude of the day was created by the fear of the impact on families that adopted children from socially and economically challenged households.

In 1912 President Taft created the Children's Bureau to investigate and to report on several child-related issues. Those issues included infant mortality, birth rates, orphanages, juvenile courts, and other social issues of that time, including adoption, a key social issue of the time.

From approximately 1912 to 1921, the practice of "baby farming" became popular throughout the United States.[20] The practice's origins are not known; however, most agree that it came from Victorian-era Britain. Baby farming was a cross between day care and selling children for profit. This practice was started to help mothers who could not care for their children. However, it turned into an often-fatal practice, as disease spread among babies in their care and abuse ran rampant. Entrepreneurs began to practice what we would consider commercial adoption, which involved turning the process into a purely money-making transaction. Those who practiced commercial adoption took on multiple children from economically and socially challenged mothers and then extracted money from the adoptive families. This was a particularly dark period in the history of adoption in America.

Minnesota became a pioneer of adoption regulation, guidelines, and procedures. In 1917 it passed a law requiring home studies, adoption confidentiality of records, and the sealing of birth certificates. This law became the precursor to what we consider today to be closed adoption.

The year 1921 was a crucial year in the history of adoption. This was the year the Child Welfare League of America (CWLA) was formed. It was made up of several different organizations devoted to providing services to and for children. The CWLA was best known for bringing a new level of professionalism to the practice of social work. It helped define multiple standards, policies, and procedures, ranging from management to placement practices and from record keeping to the establishment of formal training. Prior to the establishment of these standards, a governing body for regulating child welfare did not exist.

---

[20] The Free Dictionary, s.v., "baby farming," http://medical-dictionary.thefreediction-ary.com/Baby+Farming.

The creation, enforcement, and education of standards were at the core of the organization's reason for existence. Much of current social work owes its existence to this historical organization.

Building on the growing trend of formalizing the care of children, a series of field studies were conducted from 1919 to 1929. These studies produced the first scientific data surrounding the number of adoptions taking place. They studied what types of children —race, age, and sex — were being adopted and what types of families were adopting them. Additional studies began to dive into how children who had been adopted turned out in their new homes. Until that time, few studies had tried to measure how adopted children developed socially, economically, or morally.

Until 1935 very few studies or laws delved into the adopted child's actual rights. The Social Security Act of 1935 marked not only an expansion of foster care but also an expansion of children's rights. This act created aid for child welfare, which included dependent children. Around this time, child rights, let alone adoptee rights, were few and far between.

Prior to the twentieth century, adoption practices did not include the loss of contact between an adoptee and their biological family. The current definition of adoption would not have fit this practice well; the earlier practices would have been better described as sharing. I use the term *sharing* because contact was not cut off between the adoptee and their biological family, and interaction was frequent. The matching concept was a stark contrast to prior adoption practices, as it was designed to replace the biological family, which made contact with them unnecessary. Early matching efforts, reinforced by law, listed only religion as a prerequisite for placement. However, placement organizations often ignored this statute in order to place children in homes that were consistent with their individual religious preferences.

During this time and up until roughly 1970, the adoption practice of "matching" was popular. The term *matching* defined the practice of connecting children with families whose outward, socioeconomic, and even physical appearance matched that of the child. In other words, an adopted child would look, act, talk, and even think like a biological child in the adoptive family. The practice even went as far as mimicking intellectual capacity. More obvious requirements included racial and religious consistency between parents and children. The overall goal of matching was to create similarities and to avoid obvious differences.

The matching process was very popular among couples that could not conceive. It became so popular that infertility was a common reason for participation in matching. Use of this approach was a popular alternative to living a childless life; adoptees could easily pass as a member of the family because they bore physical, intellectual, and even religious similarities. This approach was an attempt to replicate a "natural" relationship through mostly outward appearances. Its practice reinforced that biological ties and blood relation were to be valued above all else.

This approach also sent a not-too-subtle message to the adoptee that adoption is somehow inferior, as it attempted to create the appearance of sameness and to discourage the celebration of differences. Even today there are still remnants of matching within adoption agencies regarding the issue of race. Staunch opposition to matching appears within the open adoption, international, and transracial adoption movements.

The year 1939 stands out in adoption history as a literary first. That was the year Valentina P. Wasson published the book *The Chosen Baby*.[21] It was the first book written to help parents tell their young children they were adopted. This was a brilliant approach — combining story reading

---

[21] Valentina P. Wasson, *The Chosen Baby* (New York: J. B. Lippincott, 1939).

in conjunction with age-appropriate conversations that parents had with their adopted children.

The book's emphasis was on the fact that adopted children were special because they were chosen. In addition the book included examples of home studies, interviews, and even the selection process itself. This book was unique not only because it broached the subject but also because it included quite a bit of detail surrounding the actual process. Although there are many books available today to help adoptive parents bring up the topic of being adopted, I want to share an excerpt from the story itself.

> Once upon a time in a large city lived a Man and his Wife. They were happily married for many years. Their one trouble was that they had no babies of their own.
>
> One day they said to each other: "Let us adopt a baby and bring him up as our own." So the next day they called up a Home which helps people to adopt babies, and babies to adopt parents, and said: "We wish so much to find a baby who would like to have a mother and father and who could be our own. Will you help us find one?"
>
> The Lady at the Home said: "This will be difficult because so many people wish to adopt babies and are waiting for them, but come and see me anyhow."
>
> So the Man and his Wife went to the Home and said to the Lady: "We wish so much to choose a baby. We want to have a lovely, healthy baby boy." The Lady at the Home asked them many questions and said: "I will try very hard to find a lovely baby boy, but you must wait for a long time."

A little later another Lady from the Home came and looked over the house where the Man and his Wife lived to make sure that the Chosen Baby would live in a light, clean home.

Many months went by and the Man and his Wife would say to each other: "I wonder when our baby will be coming." And the Wife would call up the Lady at the Home and say: "We are still waiting for our baby. Please don't forget about us." And she would be told not to worry, for the baby was sure to come some day.

Then suddenly one day the Lady at the Home called up and said: "We have three fine babies for you to choose from. Will you both come and see them?" So the very next day the Man and his Wife, feeling very excited, hurried to the Home. The Lady told them all about the babies.

The first baby was a little boy with blue eyes and curly blond hair. He laughed and played with a rattle. The Man and his Wife watched the baby, then they shook their heads and said: "This is a beautiful child, but we know it is not our baby." And they were taken to see the next.

And there asleep in the crib lay a lovely, rosy, fat baby boy. He opened his big brown eyes and smiled. The Wife picked him up and sat him on her lap. The baby gurgled, and the Man and his Wife said: "This is our Chosen Baby. We don't have to look any further."

Transracial adoption, now considered normal within the adoption community, first took place in 1948. This historic event was achieved when a White couple adopted an African American child in Minnesota. To put this into context, the US Supreme Court declared school segregation unconstitutional in the *Brown v. Board of Education of Topeka* ruling in 1954. In addition, Rosa Parks refused to move to the back of a Montgomery, Alabama, bus as required by city ordinance and the boycott followed in 1955. This means that the first recorded transracial adoption took place nearly seven years before these historic events. I had the honor of shaking Rosa Parks's hand, and I wish I'd had the chance to shake the hands of that Minnesota couple as well.

The year 1953 saw more attempts to bring consistency and order to the adoption process, including a national survey conducted by the Child Welfare League of America. Specific federal regulations were made through the Uniform Adoption Act. The purpose of the act was to safeguard a child's welfare, to create uniformity around the placement process of children, and to promote placement in a stable home environment regardless of which state the adoption occurred in. The central premise was that adoption offered multiple benefits, not only to the adoptee but also to the parents. Those benefits included stability: psychological, economic, and some intangibles. In addition it highlighted the benefits of adoption as it pertained to governments at the state level. The act itself listed numerous benefits ranging from consistency with federal law to legal requirements and from confidentiality to the interests of the child. Unfortunately few states ever adopted it, because it was seen as overreaching and dictating state-defined adoption processes.

From approximately 1949 to 1958, the adoption landscape greatly changed, as multicultural efforts and organizations began to have a bigger impact in the United States and around the world. In 1949 Nobel Prize winner Pearl Buck set up an agency for the adoption of American biracial children. Her motivation was that these children were considered unadoptable because of their racial status and background. Buck was herself an adoptive mother. In 1956, the charter was expanded to help find families for children living in any country. Although there seemed to always be a different Buck book lying around our house, *The Good Earth* was the one that affected me most. The story details the lives of the House of Hwang in contrast to the life of a slave.

During this same period, Congress was also working on making biracial adoption easier. In 1953 Congress acted on the growing trend of US servicemen adopting orphans during the Korean War. Congress initially approved a small number of special visas to allow adoptions to happen and later added several thousand orphan visas when they realized the number of orphans that needed to be adopted. That same year, the National Urban League Foster Care and Adoptions Project began conducting the first nationally coordinated movement to place African American children in homes.

Building on a growing need for international adoptions, the process for these types of adoptions started to gain attention and garner reports. In 1957 the International Conference on Intercountry Adoptions reported on problems surrounding international adoptions, such as a lack of regulation, review, and formal processes. Today the adoption community refers to intercountry adoptions as international adoptions. Despite widespread support in the Christian community, adoption agencies throughout the United States were largely against a popular international adoption method called adoption by proxy, which involves designating an individual to adopt on behalf of another. The key issue with the proxy was its overall lack of regulation.[22] Designating a representative within the country from which you wanted to adopt did not require social worker visits or background checks.

[22] Pam Connell, "'Proxy Adoptions' from Other Countries," Families.com, June 3, 2008, http://www.families.com/blog/proxy-adoptions-from-other-countries.

Members of the US military stationed abroad led the international adoption charge. Thousands of children were in need of adoption because, ironically, servicemen stationed around the globe had fathered children that were often rejected by their own country.[23] In addition the presence of the military in various countries allowed them to see first-hand the very real need for adoption. Many Christian organizations, such as Holt International Children's Services, were heavily involved in connecting international children in need of adoption with families in the United States and adopting international children themselves.

The majority of international adoptions were transracial in nature because the popular practice of matching proved to be difficult. The international adoption trend created multiethnic families based on love rather than on the virtues of matching or similarities. Love, the key ingredient in a successful adoption, not similarities of race, religion, or history, was the predominant belief for those adopting internationally.

Buck's books played a major role in furthering the belief that biblical love conquered all. My mom and dad always were reading her latest books and seemed to draw inspiration from the fact that Pearl Buck had adopted two children of her own. Although my parents never wrote a book, I knew that books played a big role in our household because they represented higher education. Whenever I said I was bored, the inevitable answer was "Read a book!" This period included major studies surrounding international adoption, prompted discussions of cultural sensitivity, and brought up issues of recognizing racial heritage.

Over the next three years, from 1958 to 1961, a variety of standards, regulations, and acts were passed to bring further oversight, structure,

---

[23] Margaret A. Valk, "Adjustment of Korean-American Children in Their American Adoptive Homes," *Casework Papers* (1957): 152–54, excerpt at The Adoption History Project, http://pages.uoregon.edu/adoption/studies/ValkAKACTAAH.htm.

and rights in the adoption process. In 1958 the Child Welfare League of America revised its Standards of Adoption Service, the United Nations created a declaration of child rights, and international adoption was bolstered by further standards.

The very nature of adoption has attracted various surveys, psychological studies, and efforts for society to understand the biblical pattern of adoption. Since the beginning of time, God has allowed doctors, scientists, and psychiatrists to understand more about us as His creation. In 1960, psychiatrist Marshall Schechter published his study asserting that adoption created an increase in clinical populations (a group of people that are studied for public health reasons) at one hundred times those of nonadopted people. Schechter's theory defined adoption as a risk factor for emotional health, behavioral, and educational issues, which would lead to an increased need for psychiatric counseling and care.[24]

It was psychological studies such as Dr. Schechter's that created a "scientific" link between adoption and the concept that adoptees were somehow damaged. This mind-set, established in the 1960s, changed the landscape of adoption forever. I believe this period marked the departure of a Christian worldview of adoption and began to usher in the mind-set of counseling, therapeutic adoption, and the emergence of an entire industry aimed at postadoption services. I am not aware of postadoption services existing before the mid-1950s.

In my opinion, Dr. Schechter's findings could hardly be called scientific, as the report was based on a study group of approximately 120 children seen over the course of five years. There were numerous issues with the study, including a disproportionate representation of adopted

---

[24] Anu. R. Sharma, Matthew K. McGue, Peter L. Benson "The Emotional and Behavioral Adjustment of United States Adopted Adolescents: Part 1. An Overview," *Children and Youth Services Review* 18, 1–2 (1996): 83–100.

children in the context of the total population of adopted children. In addition, his conclusion at that time was based on gathered information that was told to him by various professional colleagues.

Dr. Schechter's main theory was based on the bond that is formed between babies and caretakers, typically a parent. He theorized that there could be no substitute for the damage that separation caused during the adoption process. Within his study he concluded that even love was not strong enough to overcome the knowledge that a child somehow had been rejected by their birth parent.

The heart of this study focused on specific cases surrounding the development of a child's personality based on his or her perception of being adopted. Dr. Schechter was not alone in his theories that adoption created psychological risks. Studies had been done in the late 1930s, 1940s, and 1950s whose focal point was similar: genealogical disruption.[25] The approach that set Dr. Schechter's report apart was that it went as far as to assert that adoptees were more likely to require counseling and therapy due to neurotic and psychiatric risks. His viewpoint and studies sparked vigorous debates and were often rejected. The current versions of this viewpoint focus on the difficulties of being adopted as represented by attachment and loss issues.[26]

Given the nature of these and other studies, it is not surprising that society as a whole has accepted that adoption is a risk factor. It saddens me, however, that a large portion of the adoption community itself has accepted this judgment as well, even today. The mind-set was that adopted children were inferior in mental and educational abilities, and entire

---

[25] "Timeline of Adoption History," The Adoption History Project, http://darkwing. uoregon.edu/~adoption/timeline.html#timeline3.

[26] "Impact of Adoption on Adopted Persons," Child Welfare Information Gateway, http://www.childwelfare.gov/pubs/f_adimpact.cfm.

industries now cater to that notion, offering counseling and psychiatric drugs to cope.

I believe that this mind-set is at the heart of why we need a fundamental change in how we define, talk about, and defend adoption. The problem I have with the acceptance of this viewpoint is that it removes the presence of God from the conversation. In addition it minimizes the power of God's love shown to us and replicated by parents who adopt children.

Over the course of the next several years, many psychological and sociological studies were conducted and books written surrounding adoption. One such book, written in 1964 by David Kirk, addressed adoption from the family perspective. This book, *Shared Fate: A Theory of Adoption and Mental Health,*[27] was written by an adoptive German father of four. It was based on the experiences of approximately two thousand families who had adopted children in the United States and Canada. This was the first widely read book that delved into the adoption process from the viewpoint of the parent.

Shared Fate proposed that adoptive parents fell into two camps: infertile couples that were looked down on and decided to avoid this discrimination by pretending an adopted child was biologically theirs and those who decided to share the fate of their adopted child. In either case his work seemed to acknowledge that adoption by infertile couples did not erase the pain of infertility. Kirk called the two choices that couples made "rejection of difference" and "acknowledgment of difference."

The idea was that the rejection of differences — taking the matching approach — would eliminate the need to tell adopted children that they

---

[27] New York: The Free Press of Glencoe, 1964.

were adopted. Those who chose the second route chose to live with their doubts and fears as a parent and "shared" concerns similar to that of the adoptee. I believe these were two honest attempts to describe choices for adoptive parents. However, I also believe that there truly is a third choice to be made. That choice is that God not only has a good plan for the adopted person's life, as He says in Jeremiah 29:11, but also that adoption — His original plan for all of mankind's reconciliation — was a part of that plan.

In 1965 the face of adoption began to change once again with movement into previously uncharted areas and reinforcement of rights in others. In Los Angeles, the County Bureau of Adoptions created a program for single-parent adoptions in order to increase the number of options for hard-to-place children. In addition the Indian Adoption Project evolved into the National Adoption Resource Exchange, which later was renamed the Adoption Resource Exchange of North America, or ARENA. The project lasted from 1958 to 1967 and placed nearly four hundred Native American children.

The year 1970 marked an important statistical peak in the history of adoption: more than 175,000 children were adopted. Of those adoptions, approximately 80 percent were arranged by adoption agencies.

The "open adoption" movement gained significant momentum in 1971. Open adoption is most commonly defined as an adoption where the birth family maintains some form of contact with the adopted child and family. That was the year that the Adoptees Liberty Movement Association was established. Its mission was to abolish the existing practice of sealed records and to advocate the opening of records to adoptees over the age of eighteen. Its founder, Florence Fisher, was herself adopted and wanted to find her birth mother.

The year I was born, 1972, the National Association of Black Social Workers opposed transracial adoptions. The issue of race, identity, and adoption still remains a hot-button issue even today. The results of this opposition were not that more Black children were adopted but rather that they were not adopted at all. The period from July to December 1972 saw a ratio of 59 homes approved per 100 Black children waiting to be adopted. The other side of that picture showed that 108 white homes were approved for every 100 White children waiting to be adopted.

The bottom line was that there was a 39 percent decrease in adoptions of Black babies to White homes. Unfortunately there was not an increase of Black babies being placed in Black homes. Surveyed agencies indicated that they reverted back to the practice of placing Black babies with Black families or did not place them at all. This left countless babies in orphanages and in the foster-care system.

As a Christian, my prayer is that agencies today will take the stance that love — not the color of a person's skin — is a legitimate factor in the adoption process. I know that Dr. Martin Luther King Jr. wasn't referring to adoption when he said, "I have a dream that one day little black boys and girls will join hands with little white boys and girls and walk together as sisters and brothers."[28] One does wonder, however, what his thoughts might be on this topic. It was clear that he wanted a nation where judgment was not done by the color of skin but by the content of character. "I have a dream that my four little children will one day live in a nation where they will not be judged by the color of their skin but by the content of their character."[29]

---

[28] Martin Luther King Jr., "I Have a Dream" (speech, Lincoln Memorial, Washington, DC, August 28, 1963).
[29] Ibid.

I believe this is a good measuring stick to be used with the adoption process. I, for one, am glad that the agency, one of just twenty-two in Michigan, that placed me chose to use an approach based on love. I mentioned this earlier in the book, but I think it bears repeating. In 1972 there were just over 38,000 children placed for adoption in the United States. Approximately 1,500 Black children were placed in White homes. In Michigan there were 130 Black children placed in White adoptive homes.[30] Praise God that I was one of them!

The year 1973, just one year after I was born, has particular interest for me, as this was the year that *Roe v. Wade* legalized abortion. I am well aware that abortion probably was considered as an option for my then-fourteen-year-old biological mother. In addition I have come across many stories of young, pregnant mothers who are on their way to an abortion clinic but leave the clinic at the last moment.

For better or worse, there is a tie between abortion and adoption. I have often heard adoption positioned as the "alternative" to abortion. Given that abortion involves taking the life of a child, and adoption gives a child a new life, I like the symbolism used in positioning what adoption is all about. When I'm looking for something to be thankful about, while everything around me makes that process hard, I can certainly say that I am alive because my biological mother made the right choice. I do not question why she made that choice but am thankful that, in not aborting me, she made a loving choice.

The main discussion surrounding adoption tends to concentrate on adoptees and adoptive parents. However, in 1976 an organization called Concerned United Birthparents (CUB) was founded to provide support

---

[30] National Survey of Black Children Adopted in 1972, September 18, 1973, Viola W. Bernard Papers, Box 162, Folder 7, Archives and Special Collections, Augustus C. Long Library, Columbia University.

for all family members affected by the separation of adoption. The organization's primary focus is on providing support to those who have given up a child to be adopted.

Between 1978 and 1998, a whole series of acts, regulations, and conferences were held on the topic of adoption and protecting specific segments within the adoption community. These milestones included the passage of the Indian Child Welfare Act, financial support being provided to states through the Adoption Assistance and Child Welfare Act, and the United Nations convention on the Rights of the Child. In addition the 1993 Hague convention on the protection of children and inter-country adoption was significant. The adoption resolutions at the Hague convention were approved by sixty-six nations and were a result of the work done by the United Nations' Rights of the Child convention.

In 1994 the US federal government got involved in interracial adoption policy. The government's Multiethnic Placement Act stopped adoption agencies from discriminating against transracial adoption on the basis of race alone.[31] It went a step further in 1996 by excluding race as a means of discrimination at all. The penalty for discrimination was removal of federal funds from the adoption agency.

National Adoption Month was created over the course of nineteen years. It involved the governor of Massachusetts, Michael Dukakis, announcing an Adoption Week for his state. President Gerald Ford made adoption a national celebration, and President Reagan proclaimed the first National Adoption Week in 1984. In 1995 President Bill Clinton proclaimed November as National Adoption Month.

---

[31] J. H. Hollinger and the ABA Center on Children and the Law National Resource Center on Legal and Courts Issues, *A Guide to Multiethnic Placement Act of 1994 Amended by the Interethnic Provisions of 1996* (Washington, DC: American Bar Association, 1998).

The final two years of this twenty-year period proved to be pivotal for the adoption community. The passage of the Adoption and Safe Families Act was key, as it marked the start of a trend of a focus on adoption rather than on reuniting families. The Act was signed into law by President Bill Clinton in 1997. This update was needed based on states interpreting the 1980 version as mandating the rights of biological parents over that of a child's welfare. A lead sponsor of the bill was Senator John Chafee (R), and it had bipartisan support. However, just one year later, Oregon passed a measure granting adoptee access to original birth certificates, which was a key step in the reunification process, should an adoptee want to pursue identifying or locating his or her birth parents.

The year 2000 saw the Child Citizenship Act pass, which made adopted children who were born in another country automatic citizens upon adoption finalization. This was not the case when our family adopted my little brother from Korea. We spent all day in court finalizing Luke's naturalization paperwork. Although he fell asleep during the process, it made quite an impression on him as a toddler. Weeks after the court appearance, he was still referring to himself as "Lukey, American citizen." Also in 2000 the US government conducted its first census recognizing the status of "adopted." The census form included the designation "adopted son/daughter" as a category. This was the first time the category was included.

Information from the 2000 census revealed that there were 118,000 children waiting to be adopted between 2000 and 2004. This figure was down from 132,000. In addition the census noted that 1.6 million adopted children were minors (under the age of eighteen). An interesting statistic revealed there were 473,000 adopted children eighteen or older within the surveyed households. As of the 2000 census, approximately 2.1 million adopted minors lived in US households. The average household income showed a median income of $56,000 a year for parents with adopted children versus $48,000 for those with biological children. The figures also showed that a small percentage, roughly 3 percent, of US adopted households had adopted three or more children.

Other interesting findings from this history-making census showed there was very little difference in the percentage of adopted families throughout the United States. In other words, there was very little statistical difference between the Midwest and other regions of the United States. The data did show a significant difference in which area children were adopted from. Approximately 13 percent of all adopted children were born internationally, nearly half from Asia, with Latin America being the second largest source with 33 percent, and 16 percent coming from Europe. Korea came in as the largest single-country source of foreign-born adopted children with 22 percent.

Between the years of 2007 and 2009, three studies on adoption stand out as providing a glimpse at adoption in America. Those studies were the National Survey of Family Growth (Jones, 2008, 2009),[32] the National Foster Care Adoption Attitudes Survey (Harris Interactive and the Dave Thomas Foundation, 2007), and the 2007 National Survey of Adoptive Parents (NSAP).

These studies showed that approximately 30 percent of Americans have considered adopting, but as of 2002, only 2 percent have done so. The reports go on to say that in 2002, there were 18.5 million women ages eighteen to forty-four who had considered adoption. That number greatly diminished, however, when those women were asked whether they had taken additional steps beyond consideration. Women who had acted on their consideration came in at approximately 2.6 million.

---

[32] J. Jones, "Adoption Experiences of Women and Men and Demand for Children to Adopt by Women 18–44 Years of Age in the United States," 2008, www.cdc.gov/nchs/data/series/sr_23/sr23_027.pdf.

In addition these studies reinforced the fact that those who choose to adopt are well above the poverty level (1.5 times above), and it provided additional details. The average woman who adopted was from forty to forty-four, married, and tended to be infertile. Another major factor in adoption consideration was that they had family or friends who were adopted. I certainly can attest to that, as I have had two close friends talk to me about being adopted before they adopted their children.

The 2007 National Survey of Adoptive Parents (NSAP) provides more recent insight into the world of adoption. According to the survey, adoption in the United States is almost evenly split between private domestic adoptions, at 677,000 (38 percent), and foster care adoptions, at 661,000 (37 percent). International adoptions make up approximately 25 percent of adoptions, at 440,000. In addition the survey showed that 88 percent of adoptive parents described themselves as a "happy" couple versus 83 percent of nonadoptive parents. Nine out of ten adoptive couples said the relationship they shared with their adopted child was "very close." The same ratio stated that if given the chance, they would certainly adopt again.

According to the Office of Children's Issues (CI), part of the Bureau of Consular Affairs at the US Department of State, there were more than eleven thousand international adoptions in the United States in 2010. Just six years prior, in 2004, international adoptions nearly topped twenty-three thousand. If you are an adopted child from China, Ethiopia, or Russia, your country of origin has been in the top three countries for US adoption for several years. The decline in adoptions came from a combination of political, social, and economical factors.[33] The top US states for international adoptions are California, New York, and Illinois.

---

[33] Bureau of Consular Affairs: US State Department, Fiscal Year 2011 Annual Report on Intercountry Adoption, November 2011.

On the domestic front, the US Children's Bureau, Administration for Children, Youth and Families June 2011 data shows that there was an increase of adoptions from fifty-one thousand in fiscal year 2006 to fifty-seven thousand in fiscal year 2009. However, those figures decreased by four thousand children in 2010. The report covers adopted children, both privately adopted and from the foster-care system, and highlights that although the number declined in 2010, the proportion of adoptions to all foster-care exits matched figures from 2009.

Adoption history continues to be written as each year passes. I am proud to say that Christian leaders, laypeople, and organizations are leading the charge to reclaim and redefine adoption by calling on their members to adopt or to help fund adoptions. An excellent example is the book *Wait No More*, by Kelly and John Rosati (Focus on the Family), and the Colorado Springs–based Focus on the Family ministry of the same name. Focus on the Family's *Wait No More* is a collaboration between adoption agencies, church leaders, and ministry partners to raise awareness of and to recruit families for those waiting for permanent families.

Other leaders in adoption efforts include Pastor Rick Warren, founder of Saddleback Church and author of *The Purpose Driven Life*, who held a civil forum on orphans and adoption. Among the many esteemed experts from around the world was Dr. Russell D. Moore, senior vice president for academic administration and dean of the School of Theology at the Southern Baptist Theological Seminary in Louisville, Kentucky. He writes and speaks frequently on topics ranging from the Kingdom of God to the mission of adoption. Moore's latest book is *Adopted for Life: The Priority of Adoption for Christian Families and Churches* (Crossway Books).

This section of my book provided a brief look into the rich history of adoption. It is by no means an exhaustive examination of adoption history. I urge you to consider this the beginning of your research into key moments that have shaped our understanding of adoption today.

ABOUT THE AUTHOR

Mark Molzen was born outside of Detroit to a fourteen-year-old ninth grader and an eighteen-year-old high school dropout. At the age of three months, he was adopted into the "United Nations of Adoption," a family that included two biological children and four adoptive children of Native American, Asian American, and African American descent.

Now a spokesperson for an $18 billion, Fortune 150 Company, he received his Bachelor of Science degree in communications from the University of Utah and several professional awards for his role in communications and public relations campaigns.

He is also a Greater Phoenix Black Chamber of Commerce board member and a deacon at Bethel Church in Arizona. Molzen and his beautiful wife, Queena, have been married for twenty years and have three amazing sons.

Follow Mark on Twitter at @RU823, on Facebook at facebook.com/chosenwithpurpose and on the web at www.chosenwithpurpose.com.

Made in the USA
Middletown, DE
10 August 2022